THE FUTURE OF THE
ATLANTIC COMMUNITY

THE FUTURE OF THE ATLANTIC COMMUNITY

TOWARD EUROPEAN-AMERICAN PARTNERSHIP

Kurt Birrenbach

FREDERICK A. PRAEGER, *Publisher*
New York • London

Published in the United States of America in 1963 by
Frederick A. Praeger, Inc., Publisher
64 University Place, New York 3, N.Y.

Published in the United Kingdom in 1963 by
Frederick A. Praeger, Inc., Publisher
49 Great Ormond Street, London W.C. 1

Printed in the United States of America

This book was originally published in Germany
by Verlag Rombach & Co., Freiburg im Breisgau
under the title *Die Zukunft der Atlantischen Gemeinschaft.*

Preface

by Christian A. Herter

The Future of the Atlantic Community, by Dr. Kurt Birrenbach, is a comprehensive and compact survey of the problems involved in the building of this Community, and the necessity for doing so. Because of the progress already achieved through the Marshall Plan, NATO, and the Organization for Economic Cooperation and Development (OECD), Dr. Birrenbach remains persistently optimistic about the future, despite the remaining obstacles outlined by him with such clarity and objectivity.

All aspects of the problem of Atlantic unity—economic, political, military, and cultural—are dealt with, and dealt with in an outgoing, liberal spirit. Although Dr. Birrenbach, as a leading member of Chancellor Adenauer's party, is a fervent supporter of European and Franco-German union, there is not a trace of the idea of a "Third Force" in this book. The whole perspective and purpose is the unity of the West. Dr. Birrenbach wants a European partnership with the United States not because it is economically indispensable for a prosperous Europe, but because it is politically indispensable for world peace and freedom.

Though the political and military measures needed to strengthen NATO are probably the most immediately urgent parts of the book, the most complicated problems are in the economic field. In that area, every compromise that is worked out, however beneficial it may be to the economies of both continents, is bound to step on the toes of some powerful economic interests. Literally the whole range of these issues is canvassed, and some are discussed in detail, including the thorny question of the dollar deficit and the long-range task involved in adjusting the gold standard to the world's expanding credit demands, whose rate of growth far exceeds that of gold production.

In the political and military fields, Dr. Birrenbach's study is equally exhaustive, yet amazingly clear and condensed. He describes the points at issue in the confrontation of General de Gaulle and Secretary of Defense McNamara over the sharing of nuclear weapons; the difficulties and the importance of NATO's conventional weapons build-up; weapons standardization; integration of the NATO command structure; and the pooling of research and coordination of production so that each country will specialize in the weapons most suitable to its industry.

But Dr. Birrenbach does not stop with outlining all the problems. He also comes up with some ingenious suggestions for practical compromise solutions. He draws on the experience of the Common Market to guide us in planning for the larger goal of an Atlantic Community. He also uses his own rich personal experience as a leading industrialist who is also an active political leader and member of the Foreign Affairs Committee of the Bundestag.

The greatest value of the book lies in its usefulness as a textbook for the intelligent layman. However, education about what is really at stake and how the interests of the U.S. have become interdependent with those of Europe is a prerequisite for the long series of compromises and sacrifices on each side which the Atlantic partnership will involve. Therefore, the book's educational service is bound to contribute to constructive political action. And to understand how far such education and action is still required, we must remember that Dr. Birrenbach's outline for the future of the Atlantic Community depends wholly upon the successful negotiation of Britain's entry into the Common Market. It is, in his opinion, the first step before negotiations with the United States can even begin.

We must remember that the postwar dreams of the original architects of European Union once seemed utopian to political observers. Even after the Treaty of Rome was signed, few believed that its schedule of progressive tariff and quota cuts would ever be met. Yet, as it turned out, they were not only met but speeded up. In other words, the pressures toward union have proved stronger than the forces of disunion; and we have every right to hope that, if we persist, the trend will gather momentum and the larger dream of a true Atlantic Community will become reality.

Contents

Contents

Introduction

> We have to make up our minds to look at
> the situation from the perspective of build-
> ing the future, not of preserving the past.
>
> —JEAN MONNET

> In a world deeply split by ideological dif-
> ferences a close-knit·Atlantic Community
> seems our only hope for eventually estab-
> lishing world order based on justice and
> the consent of the governed.
>
> —CHRISTIAN HERTER

In the course of recent years, the idea of an Atlantic
Community has come more and more to occupy the con-
sciousness of the Western world. The negotiations on
NATO reform and the debates that led to the establishment of the OECD in both the NATO Parliamentarians'
Conference and the national parliaments, were directed
to the goal of making these two institutions components
of an Atlantic Community. Over and above this, President Kennedy's administration is striving to shape the
future political and economic relations between a united
Europe and North America. It is becoming ever clearer
that the Western unification movement—which started
with the establishment of the Europe of the Six and
which will continue in a second phase when Great Brit-

ain is included in the EEC and when the EFTA problem is solved—must of necessity result in a broader Atlantic Community. Disregarding the Atlantic perspective would not only jeopardize the very process of European unification, but also the results of its successful completion. For the fate of the future Europe is bound to a close alliance with the United States. Militarily, there is no room for the concept of a "third force" in the arena of the East-West conflict.

What then, does the Atlantic Community mean, and what is its true political content?

THE FUTURE OF THE
ATLANTIC COMMUNITY

Part One

GEOGRAPHICAL DELIMITATION

OF THE ATLANTIC COMMUNITY

The first question that arises is: Which countries belong to the Atlantic Community?

With regard to the postulate contained in Article 2 of the NATO treaty,[1] the concept of the Atlantic Community gained an ever-wider following in those countries that are joined in NATO. This is not mere coincidence. Over and above its framework as a classical alliance, NATO possesses a potential for integration that could become the basis for a future community. It was their awareness of a common threat on the one hand, and of a common humanistic heritage on the other, which induced these nations—in particular the highly developed industrial countries of North America and Europe—to join for the purpose of their common defense. In this regard Turkey constitutes a special case. Turkey is considered a part of Europe and has joined

[1] "The Parties will contribute toward the further development of peaceful and friendly international relations by strengthening their free institutions, by bringing about a better understanding of the principles upon which these institutions are founded, and by promoting conditions of stability and well-being. They will seek to eliminate conflict in their international economic policies and will encourage economic collaboration between any or all of them." Article 2, North Atlantic Treaty, Washington, D.C., April 4, 1949.

3

NATO because, next to the German Federal Republic, it is the country that is most endangered.[2]

When speaking of an Atlantic Community, we tend to think in terms of the partner countries of the North Atlantic Treaty Organization. But the Atlantic Community must not be limited to these countries alone. There are other European nations—particularly Austria, Ireland, Sweden, and Switzerland—with close political and economic ties to the NATO countries. The status of Spain and Finland is, for different reasons, a complicated one, and if, for practical considerations, we do not want to stretch the concept of the Atlantic Community too far, we should consider the OECD nations[3] as part of the Atlantic Community. The solution to Finland's problem must take into account that country's particular political situation.

TASKS OF THE ATLANTIC COMMUNITY

The countries of the Atlantic Community that border on the North Atlantic and the Mediterranean face a number of tasks that they can accomplish only through joint action:

1. To secure the defense of the free West against direct and indirect military aggression, attempts at infiltration and ideological undermining, and measures of economic warfare by the Communist bloc. Neutral Eu-

[2] Lord Gladwyn, *The Atlantic Community* (London, 1961).
[3] U.S.A., Canada, United Kingdom, France, German Federal Republic, Italy, Belgium, Netherlands, Luxembourg, Portugal, Turkey, Greece, Ireland, Iceland, Spain, Denmark, Norway, Sweden, Austria, Switzerland.

ropean countries—e.g., Switzerland and Sweden—are also involved in the defense of the free West, even if they do not belong to NATO.

2. To develop closer political cooperation, particularly within NATO, a task that calls for intensive harmonization of their foreign interests and for the development of greater Atlantic solidarity.

3. To coordinate their policies in the fields of economy, finance, currency, and trade, thereby making it possible to pursue progressive economic and social policies. Such coordination could guarantee high employment without inflation or balance-of-payments crises, and ensure economic growth and optimum social security.

4. To work out a wide-ranging assistance program for the developing countries in finance, economics, and trade, in conjunction with the greatest possible amount of technological and educational aid. Such measures should be undertaken in close partnership with the receiving nations.

5. To develop objective standards for sharing the burdens within NATO and the OECD—which, in NATO, should not be limited merely to the sphere of finance.

6. To promote cultural cooperation among the Atlantic nations, to increase scientific exchange in teaching and research, and to create greater understanding of the cultural values of nations throughout the world.

7. To utilize fully existing institutions and to develop new common institutions for common goals, provided that they serve the purpose of promoting Atlantic unity.

Because of the fundamental change in world politics, it has become mandatory that these tasks be mastered, and mastered jointly. Neither the defense of the Western world, nor the economic development of the countries of the Atlantic Community, nor effective aid to developing countries can be accomplished merely through the co-operation of the U.S.A. and the other countries in the Atlantic Community. The increasing interdependence between the Atlantic nations makes the further development of their common organizations and a high degree of integrated and harmonious cooperation mandatory.

THE CHANGED WORLD SITUATION

The understanding of the causes of this historical evolution and its political effects must inform measures of adjustment to the new situation. The changed world situation is manifested in the following developments:

1. The era of bipolarity in the international power structure is drawing to a close. The emergence of new power centers is leading to the gradual formation of a pluralistic order: the renaissance of the European powers as a unit; the rise of China and India; and the increasing political importance—especially within the U.N.[4]—of the third, "non-committed" world. The fact that the present leading powers will occupy a special position even in the pluralistic order of tomorrow does not denigrate the importance of this development.

[4] W. W. Rostow, *United States in the World Arena* (New York: Harper & Brothers, 1960).

2. Military-technological developments have brought the United States within the orbit of vulnerability; consequently, the world is approaching a state of nuclear equilibrium, however precarious.[5] A relative equalization of Communist superiority in conventional armed forces, necessary for the establishment of a global balance of power, must be brought about by the European nations. Thus they will play a meaningful role in the Atlantic defense system—which includes the U.S.—particularly once Europe has achieved political unification. This will hold true even though technical nuclear developments have widened the gap between the atomic power of the United States and the military potential of the European nations.

3. The economic position of the United States, powerful though it may be, has suffered, both in comparison with the Soviet Union (in terms of growth rate) and Europe (largely because of the establishment of the European Economic Community). The American economy is also more vulnerable than it has been in the past, as the acute balance-of-payments difficulties demonstrate.

4. Because of the constantly increasing volume of world trade and lagging gold production, the two leading Western currencies—dollars and pounds sterling—cannot meet the demands imposed by the international currency mechanism. The freedom of action of the U.S. and of Great Britain is thereby unduly limited.

[5] Henry A. Kissinger, *Nuclear Weapons and Foreign Policy* (New York: Doubleday and Company, 1957).

Part Two

THE REORGANIZATION OF NATO

The organizations that might facilitate the adjustment of Atlantic Community policy to new political and economic situations are: NATO, the OECD, and the NATO Parliamentarians' Conference. With regard to the establishment of an Atlantic Community, NATO in particular, if it is to survive, must be reorganized.

For many years, the member states of the North Atlantic Treaty Organization have searched for a common strategy suited to the new technological situation, a strategy based on a re-evaluation of strategic and tactical nuclear weapons on the one hand, and of conventional defense systems on the other. Unfortunately, their efforts have not yet led to common agreement. Great Britain and France particularly have impeded the formulation of a common Atlantic strategy, for both cling to an outdated idea of a national deterrent. Britain's White Paper on Defence of 1957, though somewhat modified by the White Paper of 1962, meets the requirements of a modern Atlantic strategy as little as does the idea underlying the present reform of the French armed forces. The conceptual gap between these two nations and their allies poses a serious problem, which, if left unsolved, will weaken the cohesion of NATO.

Because of the incipient nuclear stalemate, NATO's conventional forces must be increased to equalize present Soviet superiority in this field. The United States has set an example for its European allies by considerably reinforcing its forces stationed in Europe, but the task will fall mainly to the European NATO allies. In this connection, the return of the French Army—now that the Algerian problem has been solved—will be one of the most important steps toward the consolidation of military forces in Europe. The German Federal Republic, by extending the period of military service, will reach the target dates set by NATO for the German contribution more quickly. Great Britain cannot afford to ignore the example of her allies, nor can the reinforcement of the British contingent on the Continent be hamstrung by balance-of-payments difficulties. Great Britain will have to decide in the near future whether the abolition of compulsory military service is justifiable under the present circumstances.

For reasons of both absolute and gradual deterrence, the development of atomic weapons and their carriers (as well as all other means of defense) must be pressed anew, in order to prevent another Soviet "technological breakthrough" from upsetting the military equilibrium to the disadvantage of the West. The danger is particularly great that the Soviet Union might develop, on the basis of its atomic tests carried out in the last months of 1961, an effective antimissile missile and thus radically change the total balance of power. The Western world cannot afford to run the risk of such a change. Hence, regardless of criticism from the uncommitted nations, strenuous efforts must be made to prevent the Soviet Union from gaining a lead in the technology of atomic warfare. The fact that there has been no real gap so far in the field of intercontinental missiles is no reason for complacency, especially since the Soviets have a considerable quantitative and qualitative lead over the United States in the field of medium-range missiles. This lead is a serious danger for the European nations, for it makes them—as Premier Khrushchev pointed out to some Western ambassadors—"hostages" of Soviet power. The closing of the medium-range missile gap is one of the most urgent requirements for strengthening NATO. Hesitancy on the part of the United States in pushing ahead at maximum speed with the development of nuclear weapons is apparently based on the vague hope that, somehow or other, the nuclear armaments race can be halted by an agreement on controlled, world-wide disarmament. The collapse of the negotiations on the cessation of nuclear testing leaves little hope that this goal can be attained within the foreseeable future. The hopes of the Western world, including those of the German Federal Republic, will always be for a solution of the problems of disarmament that break the vicious circle of the Cold War. But Soviet intransigence continues to bar the road to agreement.

THE CONTROL OF NUCLEAR WEAPONS

Neither a strategy adjusted to military-technological evolution nor the reinforcement of nuclear and conventional forces can remove the uncertainties that beset the Western alliance. Among these uncertainties, the most harrowing is the unanswered question of the control of the use of nuclear weapons. It is the settlement of this issue that will largely determine the political fortunes of NATO.

It is necessary to differentiate between "control" in the English sense of the word—namely, the physical disposition over the use of nuclear weapons—and "control" in the French sense—namely, inspection and verification, irrespective of who is in physical possession.[1] The endeavors of both Great Britain and France to become atomic powers were prompted mainly by their desire for a greater share in the determination of "control" in the French sense rather than "control" in the sense of physical disposition. The more effective the common preparation and planning, and the likelier the possibility of strengthening the strategic conception of the United States as the guarantor of nuclear defense, the more the Allies believe themselves able to rely on the United States in an emergency. A politically and militarily satisfactory solution of this problem would greatly strengthen the effectiveness and cohesion of NATO.

The American Government has twice offered to equip the NATO powers with atomic weapons for their own disposition: first, through former Secretary of State Herter at the NATO Assembly in Paris in 1960, and again,

[1] Albert Wohlstetter, "Nuclear Sharing: NATO and the N + 1 Country," *Foreign Affairs*, April, 1961.

through President Kennedy in Ottawa in the spring of 1961. The United States offered to arm NATO with seaborne medium-range nuclear missiles. The American President made this offer contingent upon two conditions: first, that the European powers increase considerably their contribution of conventional armed forces to NATO; and secondly—and this should be self-evident —that they present proposals to the American Government for the multilateral control of a future atomic strike force that would be feasible both politically and militarily. So far, neither of these conditions has been met. It is not surprising that the European powers have failed to make good on these counts, but before discussing the ways and means of attaining the goal envisaged by the United States, it is necessary to determine whether the development of a NATO nuclear deterrent serves a useful purpose.[2]

The argument by which one or another European power will justify the creation of its own national deterrent is based mainly on the concern that the United States—aware of its own vulnerability in an atomic war with the Soviet Union and fearful of Soviet reprisals— might hesitate to use its atomic weapons in the case of an attack not directly aimed at the United States.[3] Let us note, however, that Europeans are equally apprehensive about the opposite hypothesis, namely, that the United

[2] Alastair Buchan, *NATO in the 1960's* (New York: Frederick A. Praeger, 1960), p. 57.
[3] Ben T. Moore, *NATO and the Future of Europe* (New York: Harper & Brothers, 1958), p. 7.

States would use its ultimate weapons prematurely, particularly because the conventional arm of NATO has not been sufficiently developed. In the meantime, it is becoming clear that a European power, even of the size of Great Britain or France, is not in a position to make a contribution to the nuclear deterrent of the West that would raise it substantially above American deterrent power. Today, no European power has the economic strength to carry the immense financial burden imposed by the development of an effective deterrent. This applies to both atomic warheads and the means of their delivery. It is likely that in a few years, both the English V-bombers and the French Mirage IV will no longer meet the requirements of effective retaliation against the Soviet Union. Inadequate dispersal of launching bases would make the retaliatory forces of these two nations extremely vulnerable. As far as the Soviets are concerned, short range and vulnerability deprive these national European weapons systems of their deterrent value, thus limiting their effectiveness.

There is no doubt that other political considerations have also played a role in the creation of national deterrents in Western Europe. But these are irrelevant to the argument between West and East. The skepticism toward national strategic deterrents, however, does not imply that there are no other alternatives for the development of national retaliatory forces in Europe. The question should now be phrased thus: Would the creation of an autonomous NATO strike force be likely to still the doubts of certain European powers?

First of all, it is improbable that the mere existence of a NATO nuclear strike force could compel the United States to engage in military hostilities if it did not wish to do so. Among the many possibilities for NATO-controlled nuclear forces, two extreme alternatives must be eliminated, namely, that the fifteen NATO powers together, each exercising the right of veto, or that the American Commander in Chief of NATO—SACEUR—alone should be given the power of decision. In the former case, the decision to use nuclear weapons could be thwarted by the veto even of the smallest European power, so that the use of NATO's nuclear force would be not only ineffective but also completely unlikely. Whatever the alternatives, and no matter how they are phrased, the United States cannot be eliminated as the decisive factor. Since the President of the United States will not, and according to the Constitution of the United States cannot, delegate his right of command to SACEUR, it is unthinkable that the decision to use American retaliatory power should be left to SACEUR or to all or any European NATO powers. The Soviet Union could not distinguish Polaris missiles launched by an autonomous NATO retaliatory force from those belonging exclusively to America. The use of a NATO nuclear strike force against the Soviet Union would therefore be equivalent to the decision to wage World War III.

Nor is the problem resolved by the alternative suggested by the Secretary General of NATO, Dirk Stikker, that NATO could decide on the use of nuclear weapons by a weighted "right of codetermination." In such an arrangement, the United States would still carry so much weight—consonant with the magnitude of its effort—that it could hardly be outvoted. Nor does it appear possible to create a small group of powers within NATO that would be authorized by the remaining members to use, in accordance with certain predetermined "rules of engagement," atomic weapons in the European theater. Since the United States appears to be veering away from any rules for automatic response to nuclear aggression, this solution appears impractical. In view of the magnitude of the Soviet threat, a NATO nuclear force of the size presently contemplated by the United States could only be regarded as a "trigger" that would release the Strategic Air Command and the intercontinental missiles located in the United States. The problem, then, remains the total engagement of the United States. Furthermore, the creation of a NATO nuclear force is fraught with the danger of strengthening certain tendencies in the United States to back out in the case of a Soviet attack on Europe in order to save its own population from a deadly holocaust. This is a serious contingency, which the Europeans should take into consideration.

In view of the experiences during the last Berlin crisis, one is impressed with the steadfastness of American resolution. Although Berlin—as seen from the United States—is precarious and geographically peripheral, the United States, under certain conditions, was ready to resort to nuclear weapons. If the automatic triggering of such weapons were speeded up, it would seem more practical in case of a Soviet attack for NATO to authorize the President of the U.S.A. to initiate an atomic conflict, an alternative that so far has hardly been considered.

The second argument adduced to justify European codetermination is inspired by fear: The United States, so the argument runs, must be prevented from carelessly and irresponsibly initiating a nuclear conflict. Postwar history, however, does not warrant such an insidious hypothesis. On the contrary, the United States, even when it had a monopoly of nuclear weapons, did not use it to change the world's balance of power.

If, then, a NATO strike force does not strengthen the defense of the West, but even contains elements that, under certain circumstances, are apt to weaken it, other and better arguments must be advanced to justify European claims to codetermination. There is, indeed, a plausible argument for more effective codetermination by individual NATO powers. West European powers armed with national-deterrent forces cannot stay out of a serious East-West conflict, for the first strike of the Soviet Union would be directed against them. Hence they may justly claim to exercise the right to codetermine nuclear counterattack together with (1) the United States; (2) the state that is directly threatened by a Soviet attack; and (3) the state from whose territory atomic weapons are to be launched. Furthermore, the power that fields the strongest *armée de couverture* in Europe—i.e., the German Federal Republic—should also qualify for membership in any committee deciding on the use of NATO nuclear weapons. In this regard shield and sword form an indissoluble unit. Nevertheless, there are no grounds for rescinding the pledge of the German Federal Republic, given upon its adherence to the West European Union, to abstain from the manufacture of ABC weapons.

Another strong argument in favor of a NATO nuclear force is that responsibility for use of nuclear weapons is a major factor in political integration. Since, however, the idea of "fifteen fingers on the trigger" is militarily impracticable, that solution would do next to nothing to further the political integration of NATO. And the creation of two different classes of NATO powers would lower rather than raise the spirit of the Alliance. Events would take quite a different course, however, if a European Union, once political integration is sufficiently far advanced, could form a true European Defense Community. But such a political evolution will definitely not be completed for several years. Were Europe to achieve true unity, the United States might consider transferring strategic nuclear weapons to it on condition that they only be used in partnership with the United States.[4] The United States would then remain faithful to its present policy, i.e., not to create any additional nuclear powers. Yet it must be clear that such a European nuclear force could never be a substitute for the American nuclear force. Any attempt

[4] Henry A. Kissinger, *The Necessity for Choice* (New York: Harper & Brothers, 1961), p. 126.

to create a third power independent of the United States would have dangerous consequences. McGeorge Bundy, President Kennedy's Assistant for National Security Affairs, speaking in Chicago on December 6, 1961, revealed the Grand Design: "The productive way of conceiving the political future of the Atlantic Community is to think in terms of a partnership between the United States on the one hand and a great European power on the other." This, of course, presupposes that, sooner or later, Great Britain and France will be ready to incorporate their national-deterrent forces into a collective European Defense Community. In that case, the identity of political and military will would be established, and the problem of second-rate NATO powers would be eliminated.[5]

The above considerations apply mainly to the use of nuclear strategic weapons. However, since the Soviet Union possesses strong conventional forces as well as tactical nuclear weapons, the West has no choice except to equip its armed forces with tactical nuclear weapons. Because of the necessarily decentralized structure of nuclear command in the field, NATO must devise appropriate procedures for the deployment of tactical nuclear weapons, particularly for short-range battlefield weapons. It is conceivable that, while maintaining the precedence of civilian over military power, responsi-

[5] Raymond Aron, "Une troisième puissance atomique: OTAN ou Europe," *Figaro,* February 27, 1962.

bility for the decision on the use of such weapons could be transferred to the organs of NATO itself.

THE U.S. AND EUROPE—A MILITARY UNITY

An examination of the true interests of the United States in the 1960's can lead only to the conclusion that the American stake in the use of ultimate weapons is as great as that of Europe. The loss of Europe would isolate the United States so completely that its very survival as an island of freedom amidst the Communist world would seem doubtful. The American armed forces in Europe, a substantial part of the total defense force of the U.S., play a crucial role: Any massive attack upon the European continent cannot be seen as other than the first wave of an attack eventually aimed against the United States itself.[6] The interdependence of America and Europe has now reached the point where their military and economic destinies are inseparable. The European nations would be well advised to concentrate less on American strategic weapons and more on binding the United States so strongly to a true Atlantic Union that, in the American perspective, the fate of Germany or France would not seem different from that of Alaska or Florida.[7]

However, the problem of American-European relations is primarily political rather than exclusively mili-

[6] Wohlstetter, *op. cit.*

[7] Dean Acheson, *Power and Diplomacy* (Cambridge, Mass.: Harvard University Press, 1958).

tary. Most certainly, the cohesiveness of the military alliance would be greatly strengthened were it possible to increase the conventional armed forces on the European continent to the point where the Soviet Union would be dissuaded from launching a conventional surprise attack against NATO. At present, NATO's conventional forces in Europe are not sufficient to repel such an attack, particularly since the aggressor could elect at any time to use tactical weapons, thus starting a gradual escalation of nuclear conflict. For Europe, the time has not yet come to abandon the doctrine of massive retaliation. Talk about "threshold" and "pause" appears premature, for the military requirements for so sophisticated a strategy have not yet been met. This much is clear: The use of ultimate weapons is unavoidable if Soviet aggression in Europe exceeds the dimensions of a *coup de main*.[8] The United States, too, is fully aware of this ineluctable fact.

POLITICAL COOPERATION WITHIN NATO

Closer political cooperation within NATO is the next and most important task, especially since future European contributions in conventional weapons will confer a heightened significance on the major European partners in NATO. How this cooperation can be achieved has been the subject of many studies.[9] It appears that

[8] Franz Joseph Strauss, "National Sovereignty and Alliance," an address delivered at Georgetown University, Washington, D.C., November, 1961.

[9] Lester B. Pearson, *Diplomacy in the Nuclear Age* (Cambridge, Mass.: Harvard University Press, 1958), p. 31.

the solution lies not so much in the creation of new institutions than in the will of the NATO nations to comply fully with their treaty obligations.

Anthony Eden's suggestion to create a political general staff for the coordination of Western politics deserves close attention.[10] Composed of highly qualified and experienced persons from the free nations, such a general staff would work out political directives and guidelines for Western chiefs of government. A similar proposal was adopted by the Atlantic Convention in Paris: Point 2 of the Paris declaration of January 20, 1962, contains the following recommendation:

> To create, as an indispensable feature of a true Atlantic Community, a permanent High Council at the highest political level, to concert and plan, and in agreed cases to decide, policy on matters of concern to the Community as a whole. Pending the establishment of the Council, the Convention recommends that the North Atlantic Council be strengthened through the delegation of additional responsibilities.

Anthony Eden's far-reaching suggestion must not lead us to overlook the great possibilities inherent in the already existing NATO Council. If one believes, as he does, that the imperfections of the existing institutions are due to a lack of confidence of the Western nations in their own values and a determination to live by these values, this crisis will not be overcome by creating new institutions. The problem is rather that of strengthen-

[10] Lord Avon [Anthony Eden], in *Freedom and Union* (October, 1961), pp. 3–5.

ing the existing central organ of political consultation within the Western alliance. A suggestion made by Alastair Buchan, Director of the Institute for Strategic Studies in London,[11] namely, to reorganize the NATO Council, has met with widespread interest. He proposed to separate the Offices of Secretary General and Council President and to transform the latter into the dominant political and administrative office within the NATO organization. Under it, the Secretary-General, together with four deputies, would form a Secretariat, administering the Departments of Political and Military Planning, Europe, Extra-European Affairs, and Economic Problems.

This proposal now appears as unconvincing as the one made earlier by Anthony Eden. And it is not without dangers, for two reasons: First, it would increase the possibility of excessive bureaucratization of the civilian NATO administration; second, subordinating SACEUR to a deputy of the Secretary-General—namely, the head of the Department of Political and Military Planning—would not do justice to the special position of the former as the executive organ of NATO on the one hand, and as the American President's direct military representative on the other.

If NATO is to develop common policies and strategies, and if disintegration is to be avoided, the most important NATO partners must have a voice in any de-

[11] Alastair Buchan, "The Reform of NATO," *Foreign Affairs*, January, 1962, p. 177.

cision to use nuclear weapons. This has already been discussed at length in a different context. Only if, without endangering the security of the United States, the NATO partners are informed of the true nature of NATO armament and of defense measures taken against a possible Soviet attack, and only if, without impeding deterrence and defense, they are granted the right of codetermination, can the feeling of community within NATO be strengthened. In addition, the right of codetermination and the increased duties of consultation must not be limited to the problems delimited by the NATO treaty. Consultation among NATO partners concerning the strategic defense of NATO in Africa or the Middle East must also extend to the policy of Western powers. If their alliance is to avoid serious damage, the NATO partners must agree upon a political strategy within the United Nations, and, to a limited degree, strive to cooperate with other alliances, such as SEATO and CENTO.

Of course, the European nations must not carry their demands for consultation and codetermination too far. Being a major power, the United States has commitments in other areas of the world that most European NATO countries cannot or will not support. The boundaries between consultation and political commitment are fluid, a fact overlooked by some NATO nations which desire closer consultations. Be that as it may, membership in NATO imposes on the United States a *de facto* limitation of its freedom of action in foreign policy.

There is no doubt that political cooperation within NATO can be improved by raising the diplomatic representation to it from the ambassadorial to the ministerial level. For it is very important that the NATO countries be represented in the Council by well-qualified persons of great experience and high political rank, and that simultaneously the prerogatives of the Secretary-General be greatly strengthened. A NATO Council composed of important political figures acting in concert with a strong Secretary-General would, in the long run, make the voice of NATO one of authority—heard even beyond the contractual boundaries of the Alliance. It would be particularly desirable to convene the NATO Council periodically in the United States in order to facilitate an exchange of views between the Atlantic Community and the American President, its most influential executive. It would also be wise to consider whether the functions of the NATO Council might not be expanded, so as to include the planning of general NATO policy, as well as assuming an advisory role in the formulation of NATO "rules of engagement." Of course, the powers primarily concerned, in particular the United States, will establish their own criteria for engagement. These criteria should be conveyed to the NATO Council in good time and before the onset of crisis, so that all NATO powers have a concrete idea of the roles of engagement in each critical area of world politics. To a certain extent, this procedure is already being followed in the case of Berlin, for a natural limit to consultation is set by the justified insistence of lead-

ing NATO powers that freedom of maneuver in negotiating with a potential enemy be reserved to them, and
by the United States' political and military obligations
outside NATO's sphere of influence. That this problem
is an extremely delicate one is apparent from the statement of the "Three Wise Men."[12] At any rate, in the
future the NATO Council must be granted more extensive powers if it is to become a truly coordinating
political organ.

The introduction of the majority principle and the
weighted vote has also been recommended by the Atlantic Convention in Paris, albeit in reference to a proposed permanent High Council. This suggestion, however, seems premature, for its adoption would mean
nothing less than a breakthrough to federative forms of
the Atlantic Alliance, and the nations of the Atlantic
Community have not yet developed that solidarity upon
which federative institutions must rest. The experience
of the European unification movement during the past
decade demonstrates how slow and arduous is the progress toward communal patterns.

The United States has never yet declared itself ready
to accept any significant diminution of national sovereignty. This is understandable, for the immense power
of the United States and the vastness of its world-wide
commitments do not permit comparison with its European partners. In one area, however, namely in the field

[12] Report of the Committee of the Three, in *Europa Archiv*, No. 2,
1957, p. 9562.

of nuclear policy, great inroads on the sovereignty of the Western nations are being made. The limitations to which the United States might agree were NATO raised to the rank of a nuclear power are only of relative importance, since the main instrument of retaliation would remain in the hands of the Strategic Air Command of the United States, and thus subordinated to the constitutional powers of the American Presidency.

If, in the long run, Europe attains political unification, and particularly, if the NATO members now in the EFTA become direct or indirect partners in a European Economic Community that can develop into a political community, Europe's claim to the right of co-determination will be greatly strengthened.[13] The question whether a future European political union including Great Britain should have its own nuclear force differs fundamentally from the question whether national deterrent forces are now still useful militarily or politically. An Atlantic Community would then join a politically united Europe and the United States of America and Canada in a true and indissoluble partnership.

CLOSER COOPERATION WITHIN NATO

Close cooperation within NATO is possible only if military integration extends beyond the command level. These broader areas include not only logistics and air defense, but also their standardization and the standardization of weapons, and of course the pooling of re-

[13] P. van Zeeland, "Où va l'Occident," *Revue de la Société Belge d'Etudes et d'Expansion*, November–December, 1960, p. 845.

search and arms production in member countries. Important progress could be made if such a policy were established, even though it would undoubtedly encroach on the principle of national military independence. The arguments opposed to it, although understandable psychologically, are not convincing. A rejection of integration as the organizational principle of NATO cannot be justified.

Furthermore, policies on disarmament and arms control must be coordinated with the requirements of NATO. A common policy on disarmament will have to take into account the divergent interests within the Western world. Forming such a policy will remain, for some time to come, one of NATO's greatest problems.

The creation of an appropriate organ within NATO for organizing and coordinating ideological defenses against Soviet psychological warfare—a type of warfare that the West has so far underrated—is another desirable NATO reform. And the fact that the ideological battlefield extends beyond NATO to the whole world provides another argument for freeing NATO's political function from statutory geographical limitation.

The development of criteria for a just sharing of economic burdens within NATO is equally urgent. Fair shares should be allocated, with account taken of the size of military contributions, duration of military service, financial contributions, etc., not to mention each country's political, economic, and military condition. Finally, appropriate organs for planning and carrying out measures for the defense of the free West against Communist economic warfare will have to be envisaged.

The execution of these proposed reforms will encourage the solidarity prerequisite to further development of NATO as the nucleus of the Atlantic Community. All of them, however, would lose their effectiveness if the United States, the leading political and military power of the Western world, failed to exercise leadership within NATO—leadership which in the past years has not always been apparent. This political necessity need not conflict with the growth of European-American partnership. The U.S., by virtue of its military pre-eminence, will have to carry the main burden of Western defense for a long time to come.

Part Three

THE FUTURE OF THE OECD

In recent years, the growing recognition of the need for greater Atlantic unity has been most strikingly reflected in the economic area. The rapid progress of economic integration on the European continent has prompted Britain's historic decision to seek membership in the European Economic Community. In view of the United Kingdom's role as the center of the British Commonwealth and the sterling area, this decision has obvious global implications. EEC's success has also prompted two significant steps by the United States: joining the Organization for Economic Cooperation and Development (OECD)—the transformed and broadened version of the former Organization for *European* Economic Cooperation (OEEC)—and the enactment of the Trade Expansion Act of 1962. These steps, taken in response to the formation of a huge economic bloc in Europe, set the picture of European integration at least partially in the broader frame of an Atlantic Community, with the OECD providing essential organizational machinery, and the trade legislation covering the vital prerequisites of commercial policy. Like the United Kingdom's current negotiations for membership in the Community, both these steps taken by the United

States—the first initiated under President Eisenhower and the second under President Kennedy—have world-wide implications. Reflecting a policy of closer partnership with an expanded European community, they are attuned to the demands of world-wide trade.

U.S. Secretary of the Treasury Dillon made the following statement before the Foreign Relations Committee of the U.S. Senate during the ratification debate in Spring, 1960:

> It [the OECD treaty] clearly states the basis on which the industrialized nations of North America and Western Europe are joining together and the reasons why they are doing so. It provides a simple, sturdy platform from which the OECD countries can launch cooperative and constructive action to meet the major economic problems facing us today. Yet it does not restrict or impinge upon the sovereign rights which each of the member countries is determined to preserve.

Since some European nations—for instance, the German Federal Republic—regretted that the OECD had not been organized along stricter lines (which in view of the attitude of the U.S. Congress and other European nations was not possible at the time), it was gratifying to learn from Mr. Dillon that in the American opinion "the OECD provides to a certain degree the means for converting common policy objectives into effective action." According to the treaty, the OECD has these basic tasks: the coordination of trade and development-aid policies of member countries, and the furtherance of cooperation in expanding international trade on a multilateral, nondiscriminatory basis, in accordance with the international obligations of GATT.

The plans pursued by the American Government with the OECD seem to imply more than what is found in the text of the treaty. If the economic tasks outlined at the beginning are to be fulfilled by the OECD, cooperation of its member states will have to reach a degree of intensity that was only remotely hoped for during the negotiations of the treaty. At any rate, the OECD is the only organization capable of fulfilling these tasks. The OECD must be made into a force for economic integration, as NATO is already to a certain degree in military affairs. The interdependence of Europe and the North Atlantic nations of the American continent is becoming clearer and clearer. For the United States can only carry out its global tasks, which are even more formidable than its military ones, with the help of the industrial European nations. The structural shift of economic weight between the United States and Western Europe, the imbalance in international payments, and, finally, the magnitude of the problems of economic and financial policy confronting the nations of the Atlantic Community require a re-examination of the bases of cooperation between Western Europe and the United States in economic, financial, and currency policy.

ECONOMIC AND MONETARY POLICY

The OECD treaty calls upon its members "to achieve the highest sustainable economic growth and employment and a rising standard of living in member countries, while maintaining financial stability, and thus to contribute to the development of the world economy." The fulfillment of this task is possible only if all the economic, financial, and currency policies of the Atlantic nations are effectively coordinated. Such coordination includes joint international efforts to neutralize cyclical booms and slumps, so that greater stability in the separate member economies and therefore in the Atlantic area will be achieved.

The experience of the EEC has demonstrated that the efforts of individual nations to increase their productivity and to ensure high growth rates, while avoiding inflation and difficulties in their balances of payments, can be effectively encouraged by the group as a whole. In the EEC, as previously in the OEEC, the elimination of major trade barriers other than tariffs —namely, quotas and distortions of competition in the public and private domain—has stimulated economic activity, with "multiplier" effects both within each country and internationally. A flexible, though certainly more cautious, application of these principles to the vast Atlantic zone will be an important task of the OECD.

The goals of the member countries are far-reaching. Take, for example, the 50 per cent increase in national product, the ten-year goal set by the OECD ministers in 1961. Its achievement requires an agreed upon mutual commercial policy and suitable administrative machinery to implement it. This is the clear-cut moral of European experience in economic integration. The Economic Policy Committee's subcommittee for problems of growth will occupy a critical position in the shaping of a needed well-balanced growth policy.

Similarly significant tasks arise in international monetary policy,[1] over which the International Monetary Fund has primary responsibility; but monetary policy and economic and financial policies of the Atlantic countries are insolubly linked. The Economic Policy Committee of the OECD, particularly the subcommittee for payments problems and for monetary and fiscal policies, will have to fulfill further important functions, particularly once the OECD is charged with preparing the new currency pool of the ten industrial nations belonging to the International Monetary Fund. In the opinion of the International Monetary Fund, the need for this new agreement—to augment the currency holdings of the International Monetary Fund by a total of $6 billion—resulted "not from a failure of the monetary system, but from the more comprehensive convertibility of currencies, particularly those of the main industrial countries." The agreement will enable the International Monetary Fund "to more effectively carry out its task in the international currency order in a system of convertibility which includes more freedom for short-term movements of capital." This monetary agreement also represents an element of order for the Atlantic Community, although Japan, a country outside the Atlantic

[1] Cf. Robert Triffin, *Gold and the Dollar Crisis* (rev. ed.; New Haven, Conn.: Yale University Press, 1961); and J. Rueff, "Die Gefahren des Gold-Devisen-Standards," *Neue Zürcher Zeitung*, June 27, 28, 29, 1961.

33

Community in the strict sense of the term, is one of the members.

The agreements on credit procedures are better adapted to the structure of the postwar world economy. On the one hand, they strengthen the position of European countries, and on the other, they afford credit-granting countries an opportunity to insist on a reasonable financial and monetary policy in receiving countries. The borrowing arrangements are based on an analysis of the international monetary situation, proceeding from the general agreement that the gold-exchange standard has proved its value as a system and need not be changed.[2] Accordingly, it will suffice to make arrangements to counteract undesirable short-term movements of capital resulting from crises of confidence, differential in interest rates, or political conditions.

The existing agreements seem adequate to counteract these wayward capital movements and strengthen the effectiveness of the corrective forces tending to adjust the balance-of-payments position of both debtor and creditor countries. Furthermore, they create a firm institutional framework to supplement the highly desirable cooperation of central banks and enable them to assume tasks that could be handled only with difficulty by a voluntary cooperative effort, e.g., the Basel Central Bank Agreement.

[2] E. M. Bernstein, "The Adequacy of United States Gold Reserves," *American Economic Revue,* V, 1961.

However, the new monetary agreement fails to solve a number of problems—such as the possible scarcity of long-term reserves—because with the rapid growth of world trade, annual international exchange transactions have increased three to four times as fast as the monetary gold supply. Within the framework of the gold-exchange standard, this reserve shortage is all the more threatening, because the short-term holdings of dollars and sterling—which apart from gold form the most important component of world currency reserves—have reached their utmost limit. Two factors in particular might endanger the liquidity of the gold-exchange standard: a decrease of official foreign-exchange reserves on the one hand, and extensive private hoarding on the other. Both these factors are influenced, at least in part, by the uncertainty over the existing price of gold. Although the Government of the United States has repeatedly stated that, for political reasons, it is unwilling to change the price of gold, it has also refused to give a gold guarantee on official dollar holdings.

In the course of developing the EEC into a true economic union, the six European partner countries will have to deal with the problem of administering the currencies of member countries in a more centralized manner than is done today. Jean Monnet's fundamental idea is to start now with the pooling of at least part of the European monetary reserves. If the negotiations on the admission of Great Britain to the EEC prove successful, this problem will be even more urgent, since the British economy will not be able, in the long run, to bear sole responsibility for the stability of the sterling-area currencies. But if the British currency were backed up by all European currencies, the problem could be solved more readily. The increasing importance of European —particularly Continental—monetary reserves in the International Monetary Fund is reflected in the operating terms for the new currency pool. Although connected with the International Monetary Fund, it is given considerable autonomy.

If this development results in the decentralization of the International Monetary Fund—and the formation of the Currency Club of the Ten represents a significant step in this direction—it is conceivable that a regional European reserve center for a European federal-reserve system could develop along with successful European economic integration. Such a European federal reserve system could be instrumental in eliminating the present monetary structure that has tended toward sterling crises and structural weaknesses in the pound sterling.

In the next and last phase, the European Monetary Agreement could be converted into an Atlantic Monetary Agreement by the inclusion of the United States and Canada. The European Currency Agreement contains a guarantee for foreign-currency holdings, particularly dollar holdings, of the central banks which are partners to the agreement. If, in joining the European Monetary Agreement, the United States were to give a dollar guarantee for official dollar holdings, it would thereby protect all legitimate dollar holdings against any increase in the price of gold.

This would definitively eliminate the great danger to the liquidity of the gold-exchange standard. Thus, increasing liquidity to meet the needs of a constantly increasing world trade volume would become a technical rather than a political problem, and one that could be solved with comparative ease by an Atlantic Monetary Community once all problematical factors pertaining to dollars and pounds had been eliminated. The crucial developments of the immediate past have made obvious the close connection of monetary, economic, trade, and financial policies, and there can be no doubt that monetary policy can be coordinated only after the successful coordination of economic, trade, agricultural, and financial policies. At present, the OECD, and more specifically the economic committees within the OECD that deal with these pertinent problems, constitute the organizational framework for solving this problem. Since these committees were established, the United States has demonstrated that it is willing to make the OECD the center of these coordinating efforts. This represents a giant step toward a true Atlantic economic community.

COORDINATION OF DEVELOPMENT POLICY

The first—and for the time being the most important —task of the OECD is the coordination of Western development policy. On the basis of the experience of the

37

great Western industrial countries in recent years, one can gauge the enormous efforts the Western world will have to make to do justice to the central task of aiding the underdeveloped countries. The multilateral development of this complex necessarily moves in the direction of international financial coordination of all development policy. For this, the Development Assistance Group (DAG) forms the appropriate frame. Such coordination is essential, if for no other reason than that without coordinating financial and economic assistance —whether it is public or private—large-scale misinvestments and continual balance-of-payments crises will be unavoidable. This does not mean that development assistance should be channeled *only* through multilateral organizations—although this is desirable in the financing of important projects without which many young nations could not carry out constructive investment programs. Competition with the Soviet Union in these countries is another reason for the coordination of efforts by the Atlantic countries.

Of paramount importance—and so far this has not been sufficiently recognized—are the tasks connected with technical aid and the problem of assistance to developing countries in organizing their educational systems.

The most difficult and painful task, however, that Western countries face in relation to the developing countries is undoubtedly in the realm of trade policy. The one-way flow of capital into developing countries requires a trade policy that creates outlets for their industrial products in the markets of highly industrialized countries. Such a trade policy demands far-reaching changes in the economic structure of the Western World. Such changes, to be effective, would have to be based on joint coordinated efforts.

A classic example of a problem to be solved by a common Western development policy is that of reducing fluctuations in raw-material prices. Any solution will necessarily involve exercising an influence on investments and production in the developing countries. Here, too, the experience of the past has demonstrated how extraordinarily difficult this task is. A strengthened Atlantic Community, however, would entail the formation of a quasi monopoly of demand for raw materials in the West, and such a quasi monopoly would be of a magnitude that the countries producing raw materials simply could not ignore, even in the planning stage. This serves to illustrate why the entire development problem must be solved in close partnership with the developing countries themselves. A certain control of the demand for raw materials—possibly on the basis of long-term agreements in connection with compensation funds and buffer stocks—will help to diminish or eliminate what today is perhaps the greatest obstacle to economic development in the new countries, and thus in the world market. Only coordinated action by the West can ultimately force the Eastern bloc to refrain from interfering with efforts at stabilization, or lose face in the eyes of the developing countries. This is the greatest challenge to the Western world since the Marshall

Plan, and by far exceeds that challenge in both difficulty and scope.

THE TASKS OF TRADE POLICY

As defined by the treaty, the third task of the OECD —"to contribute to the expansion of world trade on a multilateral, non-discriminatory basis in accordance with international obligations"—appears at first sight to be only a repetition of the GATT principle.

Developments in recent years have shown that economic regionalism may lead indirectly to a world-wide reduction of tariffs. United States and Canadian membership in the OECD will enable those two countries to bring their influence to bear on the tariff structure of the future European trade system, in the direction of eliminating autarchical tendencies and promoting the GATT principles of a maximum degree of free world-wide trade. This, however, presupposes successful European integration. Restrictive trade policy practices, whether in Western Europe or in the United States, could have catastrophic effects on the entire policy of the free West. But here, too, it is evident on the basis of past experience that tariff policy is inseparable from economic and trade policies. If the European nations not only reduce their reciprocal tariffs, but also decide in favor of a low overseas tariff, the United States may adopt a policy of permanent close cooperation with Western Europe in the matter of customs.

The recent agreement between the EEC and the United States has brought to a successful end the so-called "Dillon round" of negotiations in GATT. This is a remarkable step toward a world-wide liberalization of trade policy, based on tariff reduction by the most important industrial countries of the West. For agriculture, the results are less gratifying, though not without interest.

ATLANTIC TRADE PARTNERSHIP

On October 11, 1962, the President of the United States signed the Trade Expansion Act of 1962. The new law supersedes the Reciprocal Trade Act, which, until its expiration on June 30, 1962, had been the basic charter of United States foreign-trade policy since 1934. The President has called it the most important international economic legislation since the Marshall Plan. It is of historical importance both to the development of world trade and to the relations of the United States with Europe.[3] It gives to the President three important powers:

1. to reduce existing tariffs for all countries on a reciprocal basis within a period of five years by 50 per cent, not only item by item, but across the board (i.e., for whole categories of goods);

2. to make agreements with the European Economic Community on customs reductions and customs exemptions for all those groups of products in which

[3] Jacob K. Javits, "U.S. Foreign Trade Policy," Speech delivered before U.S. Senate (Congressional Record, 87th Cong., July 10, 1961); and George W. Ball, "On the Threshold of a New Trade Era," Speech delivered before National Foreign Trade Convention on November 1, 1961.

the U.S. and the EEC together provide 80 per cent or more of world exports;

3. to exempt partially or completely from customs and other restrictions the import of tropical agricultural products from friendly developing countries.

This American policy was sponsored by Under-Secretary of State George W. Ball.

It is hoped that these measures will lead to a trade partnership between the United States and Europe.

This Atlantic partnership will then comprise almost 90 per cent of the productive capacity of the highly industrialized countries of the free West and will open the markets of the free world to this capacity. The central provision, as far as Europe is concerned, is the second one, which will affect approximately $2 billion of American exports to the expanded EEC area and $1.4 billion of American imports from the European area—including the most important products of the automotive, machinery, and chemical industries.

The President insists that any reductions agreed upon between the EEC and the United States and Canada be on a reciprocal basis, in accordance with the usual most-favored-nation provisions of GATT, and thus also benefit countries not included in the planned partnership. In view of its traditional economic relations with those outside areas, the United States cannot ignore the GATT principle. As a result, the United States, which could be shut out from the European market through the common tariff of the EEC would not suffer economic damage, and the European market would be opened for American industry just as the American market is open to Europe.

If the tariff measures suggested by President Kennedy can be carried out in accordance with his plans for progressive reciprocity, solving the problem of relations between both Commonwealth nations and the remaining EFTA countries with an all-European Common Market will be made far more easy. For the more liberal the trade policy of the EEC to begin with, the simpler it will be to solve the difficulties that would arise when the United Kingdom, as a member of EEC, is compelled to subscribe to common community tariffs enforced against nonmembers like the Commonwealth nations. On the other hand, Europe must make it clear that an autarchic agricultural policy would in the long run encounter massive resistance in the United States, thus endangering the existing economic and political ties between that country and Europe. The American Government is making courageous attempts to reduce drastically its agricultural—particularly grain—surpluses by limiting the areas under cultivation. However, the productivity of American agriculture is such that even with limited acreage under cultivation there will still be surpluses. These can, of course, be used in part for development aid, but Europe must realize that it must remain open for a reasonable, to be agreed upon, share of American and Canadian farm exports. The President clearly recognizes that this free-trade arrangement between the American and European markets is only possible if all quantitative restrictions upon a free exchange of commodities are simultaneously abolished. The history of European economic unification demonstrates that this is not possible without institutions guaranteeing fair trade and eliminating both public and private distortions of competition. The American Government also has made it clear that such a far-reaching liberation of trade from all tariff and quantitative restrictions is only possible if economic, trade, and monetary policies are coordinated among all the partners—the United States, Canada, and a united Europe. This is the particular task the OECD faces, and its Economic Policy Committee, its Subcommittee on Balance of Payments, and its Trade Committee will and must do justice to it.

For emergent Europe it is cause for great satisfaction that the United States sees Europe as its partner. The President's address to Congress of January 25, 1962, was aimed not just at the Congress, nor merely at the United States, but rather at a united or to-be-united Europe as well. Thus a great opportunity is offered to the Western world. The irrevocable abolition of trade obstacles in the European and North American markets could spur technological development in the Atlantic Community and promote a widespread specialization of industries. The forces of competition could strengthen and, at the same time, counteract inflationary developments through an increased interdependence of markets. The economy of the Atlantic area could develop dynamic forces to spur higher productivity and increased eco-

nomic growth, making possible the fulfillment of social needs to a hitherto unimaginable extent.

In this connection, it may be asked whether or not
the implementation of President Kennedy's suggestions
would lead to the disintegration of the EEC. The an-
swer to this question is: No, it will not.

Inner cohesion and solidarity in the EEC are not
based solely on a common external tariff. This is only
one—though an important one—of the instruments of
integration that forge the economic union of the EEC
members. Of much greater importance are the members'
common trade, fiscal, agricultural, economic, and, ultimately, monetary policies. The unification and harmonization of the tax and legal systems are also vitally
important. Of course, a *low* external tariff, which is the
goal of the Community's liberal trade policy, is not as
effective an instrument of integration as would be a high
protective wall. But high protective tariffs are neither de-
sired nor even possible in the present world situation.
As long as principles of reciprocity, sanctity of contracts,
and institutional safeguards of fair trade are assured,
European nations will display that understanding for
American interests to which Americans, in view of their
past sacrifices and their attitude toward the future, are
legitimately entitled. This is only consistent with the
idea that the Atlantic Community, which so far has
found its most concrete expression in NATO, is meant
seriously as the basis for the survival of the European
nations in the East-West conflict.

The far-reaching tariff authorizations granted the President under the new Trade Expansion Act are likely to prove decisive and revolutionary for the Atlantic area. The resulting across-the-board tariff negotiations between the EEC and the United States will have to be laid down in an agreement expressing a partnership in trade policy between the United States, Canada, and the Common Market.

Sooner or later, as a logical consequence of the effect of the Trade Expansion Act on monetary policy, the United States will join the European Currency Agreement, which then will assume the character of an Atlantic Monetary Agreement. The liberation of trade within the Atlantic Community from most customs and quota restrictions, the coordination of the economic, trade, and agricultural policies, and the elimination of balance-of-payments difficulties will enable the Western world to carry on the type of aid program for developing countries that will do justice to the historic importance of this task.

WILL THE UNITED STATES JOIN THE COMMON MARKET?

In a memorandum entitled "A New Look at Foreign Economic Policy,"[4] written at the end of 1961, former Secretary of State Christian A. Herter and William L. Clayton, creator of modern American trade policy in

---

[4] Christian A. Herter and William L. Clayton, *A New Look at Foreign Economic Policy* (Washington, D.C.: Government Printing Office, 1961), p. 8.

the 1930's, went much further. They suggested to the Foreign Economic Policy Subcommittee of the Joint Economic Committee of the Congress that the United States develop a trade partnership with the European Common Market and join the Common Market. In this common Atlantic market of highly industrialized countries, half a billion consumers would enjoy the highest standard of living in the world.

Since GATT excepts only customs unions and free-trade zones from the most-favored-nation principle, only these can be considered for an Atlantic Common Market. Preferential zones have to be eliminated as a matter of course. Theoretically, there are no fundamental reasons to exclude an Atlantic customs union *a priori*. There would be no insurmountable problems with regard to the union's common external tariffs. American tariffs on industrial products are generally somewhat lower—and in some instances, e.g., automobiles and agricultural machinery, even considerably lower—than the common tariffs of the EEC and of Great Britain. So are American customs on important industrial raw materials such as coal and steel. The same is generally true in regard to duties on machinery and durable goods. On the other hand, United States duties on nondurable consumer goods, particularly luxury items, are much higher than those of the EEC and Great Britain, and the duties on many chemical products are also higher than in the EEC. On the whole, the differences are not so great that they could not be adjusted in the long run. In the long run, an adjustment of these three customs systems on industrial products and goods therefore seems conceivable.

The theory of free trade is as applicable to an Atlantic union as to a European union. If the exception from the most-favored-nation principle were to become the rule, GATT would probably not survive the formation of a broad preferential system. For this reason, a general assertion on the theoretical possibility of an Atlantic union in conformity with GATT is only conditionally correct. The development of the EEC has demonstrated that a common foreign-trade tariff and the internal abolition of customs alone are not sufficient to create a common market. The realization of a common market presupposes the free movement of merchandise, persons, and capital, which in turn necessitates a common economic and trade policy of the countries joined in such a union. Adjustments in policies geared to the whole economy—such as business-cycle and monetary policy—are relatively simple. Great difficulties arise, however, when different governmental policies exist in sectional markets—such as those for farm products, transportation, or power production. The demand for a common Atlantic agricultural policy clearly reveals the problematical nature of an Atlantic common market. An Atlantic common market for farm products would endanger vast sectors of European agriculture. Similar problems arise with respect to certain industrial raw materials, e.g., coal, oil, and ore.

The question of the United States' joining the Eu-

ropean market appears incomparably more complex
from the perspective of the United States. In 1960, the
United States exported $6.3 billion to the Common Mar-
ket and imported $4.2 billion, but this amounts to only
one-third of American foreign trade. During the same
period, two-thirds of the exports went to areas other
than the Common Market: about $3.7 billion to Canada,
$3.6 billion to the Far East, $3.4 billion to Latin America
and $1.3 billion to Africa and the Middle East. A com-
mon tariff of an Atlantic Common Market therefore
would cut off the United States from areas such as Latin
America or Japan, whose economic well-being depends
on the United States. Almost one-half of South America's,
more than 30 per cent of Japan's, and more than one-
half of Canada's exports are shipped to the United
States. Restricting these exports by a common external
tariff directed against the countries traditionally linked
to the United States would be a serious, even fatal,
economic blow to them. Moreover, a power like the
United States, whose interests are spread across every
continent and every sea, cannot, by reason of its position
as the protector of the free world, submit to the majority
decisions of an economic union whose economic, trade,
and financial policies are designed for a more restricted
area.

Can this ever change? First of all, there is the understandable reluctance of the United States to shut itself
off from other areas of the world. If she did, it would be
necessary to make special arrangements for agricultural
produce, to reduce drastically the duties on raw mate-

rials, and to try to find a suitable tariff for the critical exports of finished products. For Latin America exports mostly foods and raw materials, and Japan's exports and a considerable percentage of Canada's exports to the United States consist of finished products. However, the question of whether the United States would be willing to renounce its sovereignty to the extent required in joining an EEC expanded into an Atlantic Economic Community would still remain. At the present time, such action by the United States as a step toward an Atlantic union would seem premature.

The conclusion of a free-trade agreement between the EEC, the United States, and Canada is unacceptable for the same reasons that the Maudling negotiations foundered. The extensive trade and production dislocations that such a system would entail would not be economically feasible. The kind of tariff agreement acceptable to small countries, based on certificates of origin and equalization levies, is impossible, because of the enormous trade volume of the United States.

Is it possible to impose a tariff on selected groups of merchandise—such as raw materials or certain finished products—common to the United States and Europe, while leaving other items free of duty and making special regulations for farm products, creating thereby a common market with mixed customs-union and free-trade elements? Such a solution presupposes certain common institutions that are indispensable to any type of economic union. But although this approach would run into precisely the same obstacle, it might possibly be a step toward the proposal recently made by the Government of the United States. But the road to this goal is a long one.

The very significant American initiative shown in joining the OECD and passing the Trade Expansion Act must be matched and supported by the European countries, with due recognition of their legitimate interests, if they do not want to betray the objectives of European integration. Europe's identity can and should be wholly preserved within this development. The European and United States governments are fully aware of this. If North America and Europe cooperate to strengthen their already existing economic ties, a community of independent nations united by vital interests and a common history, as envisaged by the Atlantic Convention, may still come to pass.

Part Four

NATO PARLIAMENTARIANS' CONFERENCE

If the development of an Atlantic community is successful, NATO and the OECD need parliamentary control. This development certainly should not be rushed, but the NATO Parliamentarians' Conference should be seriously examined.

The Atlantic Convention proposes "to develop the NATO Parliamentarians' Conference into a consultative Assembly which would review the work of all Atlantic institutions and make recommendations to them." This Assembly would meet regularly, or at the call of its president, to hear reports from the secretaries-general of other Atlantic bodies. Its members would be selected by member governments in accordance with the latter's constitutional procedures. They would not necessarily have to be parliamentarians. Moreover, these members would have the power to elect a limited number of additional members of equal status.

The establishment of such a parliamentary or para-parliamentary institution by means of international treaties and not—as the NATO Parliamentarians' Conference was—by private initiative would be an important step toward the consolidation of a true Atlantic Community. For the time being it would not matter too much if its prerogatives were limited to consultative functions.

ATLANTIC CULTURAL POLICY

A community such as the Atlantic Community, which is not primarily based on geographical, military, economic, or political principles, but rather on a common cultural heritage, cannot be strengthened unless it makes the development of this common cultural heritage the keystone of its policies. It has been the particular merit of the Atlantic Convention to formulate practical recommendations in the field of cultural policy; their practical realization remains one of the most pressing tasks for the Atlantic Community. According to these recommendations, an Atlantic Council, consisting of ministers of education, ministers for scientific affairs, cultural and educational authorities, and representatives of universities and scientific research organizations, should

1. determine the comprehensive aims of an education likely to promote the ideals and purposes of the Atlantic Community;

2. organize a bold Atlantic plan for youth and education with the aim of furthering the study of languages and the widest possible exchange of students, teachers, and youth leaders, as well as workers in industry and agriculture;

3. organize a program of cooperation in teaching and

research among the scientific institutions of member countries.

Individual measures likely to serve these purposes should be carried out cooperatively by all Atlantic nations within a specified period. The development of cultural institutions should be the subject of investigation by the first Atlantic Council, which, by forming subcommittees in various scientific and educational fields, should declare itself in permanent session. Thus a motive force would be created to encourage a development that, on a smaller scale, is already beginning to take shape in the European Community. Mention should be made of the large number of student-exchange programs; cooperation among European universities; the Conference of European Ministers for Cultural Affairs; and the contemplated founding of a European university. All these measures could strengthen the cultural ties linking the Atlantic peoples to the Atlantic Community without impairing the nature of specifically European interests. Atlantic cooperation in science and research would stimulate the extraordinary creative powers latent within the Atlantic Community. The task is to organize the intellectual and cultural resources of the Community in a form worthy of its common heritage.

CONNECTION WITH OTHER REGIONAL GROUPS

The stronger the ties within the Atlantic Community become, the more important becomes the problem of its relation to other regional groups in the free world and to the universal political organization of the United Nations. Relations between the Atlantic Community and other regional institutions of the Western world are particularly significant, because other nations still outside the Atlantic Community share its heritage, particularly its common Western humanistic tradition. It is obvious that the Atlantic Community—as is all of Western society —must be open to all nations with the same ideals and origins.[1] It must also be able to lay down conditions for admission that will preclude any possibility of disintegration. Some of the countries in the Atlantic Community are members of NATO, which means that they have entered defensive military commitments against attacks by third powers, whereas another group of members is unwilling to renounce its traditional neutrality. Thus we see that the structure of the Community is not uniform, that its members are differentiated by the degree of their integration, since it is organized, as it were, on the principle of concentric circles.

The future position of the British Commonwealth and the French Communauté in the Western world is being studied by the framers of European unification policy. The relation that the Europe of tomorrow will establish with these communities might serve as a model for the relationship of the Commonwealth and Communauté to the other members of the Atlantic Com-

[1] Cf. Ludwig Erhard, *Europäische Integration und Atlantische Gemeinschaft* (Lecture delivered at the School of Business Administration, St. Gallen, Switzerland, January 15, 1962) (Press Report No. 95, German Federal Ministry of Economics, January 30, 1962).

munity. Any discussion of this question must start with the fact that the free world has a basic interest in the continued existence of the Commonwealth. Commonwealth membership of the major Asiatic and African nations is a primary factor for international peace. The isolation of the so-called "former white dominions" that are related to Great Britain would be unreasonable and unjustifiable. To maintain the ties between nations formerly in the French Communauté in Africa and Europe is, from the standpoint of European self-preservation, imperative. Great Britain's admission to the European Economic Community necessarily presupposes an economic arrangement with the countries of the British Commonwealth. In the same manner, the European Economic Community wants, for political and economic reasons, to enable the young nations of the Communauté, as well as those African nations that no longer are part of it, to associate themselves with the emergent Europe. Great Britain's membership in the European Economic Community—a prospect that has become more and more likely during the past year—need not endanger the existence of the Commonwealth if the British preferential system can be replaced by economic measures of a more or less permanent nature, without thereby endangering the cohesion of the EEC. In order to preserve GATT, still the Magna Charta of world-wide free trade, these measures should not be in the nature of a new preferential system. In another connection we have pointed out why the European Economic Community is not now in a position to conclude a customs union or a free-trade-area agreement with overseas countries such as Canada, Australia, or New Zealand. The same factors militate against the premature creation of an Atlantic Common Market.

The problem of the young African nations is quite different. The existence of two preferential zones side by side in Africa—the French and the British—is untenable in the long run. Yet the fusion of these two zones is only a temporary measure. Assisting the young nations in building diversified economies—economies not based on monocultures exclusively—is even more important than maintaining preferences. Such assistance will help further internal economic growth and decrease their dependence on the world market. The reorganization of these economies will require liberal educational and financial aid for some time to come, and this assistance is more important than questionable preferential agreements.

Although the incorporation of Great Britain into the European Economic Community will increase discrimination—authorized by GATT—against American exports, acceptance of this development is an act of extraordinary political farsightedness, for it furthers the political aims of European institutions. The position of the United States is all the more farsighted because the United States itself is the victim of constant balance-of-payments crises and therefore compelled to exert special efforts to increase its exports. On the other hand, the establishment of a regional economic union such as the

EEC means an extraordinary increase in economic potential, whose positive effects take the form of increased imports of raw materials and finished products. The unity of the European market is a policy imperative, quite apart from foreign-policy commitments, else countries like Austria, Sweden, or Finland might be drawn into the Eastern trade sphere. Any association of these countries with the European Economic Community must therefore take into consideration the legitimate interests of the European countries without weakening the structure of the Community. Since Britain has made its affiliation with the European Economic Community dependent on a constructive solution of the economic problems of the countries of the Commonwealth and the EFTA zone, the European economic problem cannot be considered solved until this condition has been met. Such a solution should be greatly facilitated by the United States Trade Expansion Act of 1962, for many or most of the more complex problems in the relationship of the Commonwealth and EFTA countries to Europe could be solved in an Atlantic framework, without endangering the EEC. Europe, Great Britain, Scandinavia, and the areas to be associated with the European Economic Community could be incorporated into one Atlantic Community, all participating in constructive common trade and economic policies, with the OECD forming a provisional organizational superstructure.

The ties between the United States and Latin America forged by the Organization of American States are greatly strengthened by the Alliance for Progress. The extraordinarily significant exchange of goods, people, and ideas between Europe and Latin America will make it easier for the United States to play a decisive role in both continents without conflicting with either one, provided Europe's foreign-trade and customs policy does not shut itself off from the traditional markets in Latin America. In the interest of their own political security, the European nations must contribute—beyond the requirements of traditional bonds—to the development of the Latin American economy together with the United States. The European heritage of the Latin American nations and their strong cultural ties with Europe offer Europe, and particularly the united Europe of tomorrow, the opportunity of strengthening the bonds with Latin America. If the European nations realize the importance of this objective, the Western world need not worry about South America's alignment in the East-West conflict.

As to relations between the North Atlantic Community and the United Nations, there is no doubt that this is an area in which conflicts during the past years have repeatedly endangered the existence of the Western alliance. The course followed by NATO nations in the U.N. has created the impression that their cooperation is limited to the defense of Europe. But, as pointed out before, it is no longer justifiable to limit cooperation to this one task; in the next few years, the nations of the Atlantic Community must develop a common policy within the U.N., or at least coordinate their policy within that body, lest it become completely dominated by the Eastern bloc and the Afro-Asian countries. Such a development would be contrary to the universal character of the United Nations, let alone the political interests of the Western alliance. The Atlantic countries, were they united in a true political community, would be a major stabilizing element in the U.N., thus putting to an end the disunity of the free world that has been so apparent in the U.N. during the past years. An Atlantic Community granting large-scale and long-term development aid would exercise great attraction on the "non-committed" world. Because of its compass, and because it will be extended with a realistic understanding of the young nations' neutrality in the East-West conflict, this aid would differ conspicuously from that granted by the Eastern bloc, which could therefore be forced either to support the aims of the U.N. or reveal itself publicly to the whole world as the destroyer of the U.N. If these goals—closer political union and coordination of development-aid programs—are attained, it will be possible to conceive of an Atlantic Community comprising, in different degrees of integration, the twenty nations of the OECD, while maintaining close political and economic ties with Latin America, Africa, the Middle East, the countries of the Commonwealth, and Japan.

Part Five

The question of the increased commitments to the West made by the Federal Republic raises a counterquestion concerning the consequences of such a policy in regard to Germany's rightful claim to reunification. The signatories of the Treaties of Paris and Rome have agreed that since a reunited Germany would not presumably be identical with the Federal Republic, they would have the right, in keeping with the precedents of international law, to reconsider the terms of their association. The question of review has not been the subject of a formal reservation in any of the relevant treaties, with the exception of Article 10 of the Treaty on Germany of May 26, 1952, as amended by the Protocol of October 23, 1954, on the Termination of the Status of Forces in the German Federal Republic, and the declaration of the head of the German delegation on February 28, 1957, concerning the question of the applicability of the Rome Treaties on Germany after her reunification.[1] In accord with the Western allies, the

[1] Wohlfarth-Everling and Glaesner-Sprung, *Kommentar zum Vertrag der Europäischen Wirtschaftsgemeinschaft* (Berlin and Frankfurt a.M.), p. 585. The commentary states: "It [the Declaration] leaves the possibility of the participation or nonparticipation in the treaties by the

British Foreign Secretary, Sir Anthony Eden, acknowledged the legality of this situation in his declaration to the House of Commons on November 28, 1954.[2] Neither the treaty for the establishment of the West European Union nor the North Atlantic Treaty provides a revision clause applicable to a reunified Germany. Yet the same considerations that apply to the Rome Treaties apply also to the WEU Treaty and the Atlantic Pact, for the reunification of Germany would transcend a mere territorial change as it is defined in international law.[3] More important still, the Western allies, in Article 7, Paragraph 2, of the Treaty on Germany, have made German reunification a foreign-policy objective. Thus, the reunification of Germany—the natural right to self-determination of a free nation—is indissolubly linked to the policy of the most important countries of the Atlantic Community. The Federal Republic, and also a future

reunited Germany completely open. The Declaration is in agreement with the opinion of the Federal Government that a reunited Germany must have complete freedom of political action concerning treaties concluded before with respect to a part of Germany. No objection was raised against this Declaration by the other parties of the treaty. It has been confirmed by several statements, particularly by French politicians; among others, it is expressed in the report of the Defense Committee of the French National Assembly (Publication No. 5367): "Le Traité nous engage définitivement mais n'engage pas l'Allemagne de l'Ouest, qui conserve la liberté de choisir, de partir ou de rester, le jour de sa réunification." (The Treaty obliges us definitively but does not oblige West Germany, which preserves the freedom of choosing to leave or to stay, on the day of her reunification.)

[2] House of Commons, Official Report, November 28, 1954, vol. 533, col. 688.

[3] Wilhelm G. Grewe, *Deutsche Aussenpolitik der Nachkriegszeit* (Stuttgart, 1960), pp. 103, 185.

reunited Germany, must and will be firmly committed to the West.

Securing self-determination for the entire German nation remains a vital objective of German policy. If the German Federal Government does not tackle it with all its might, within the limits of the possible, we can rest assured that the rulers of the zone behind the Iron Curtain and the Wall will adopt the slogan of reunification —with signs reversed. The German nation must face any risk short of losing its freedom and severing its ties with the West to secure the liberation of the Soviet Zone. To some, this determination may appear to pose a dilemma, yet as a nation, Germany has no other choice if it wants to live in freedom. Since the very existence of the German Federal Republic is threatened unless it is supported by the West in this task, Article 7, Paragraph 2, of the Treaty on Germany will continue in force. This provision bars recognition of the Soviet Zone by Germany's allies or partners. The controversies over Berlin during the past months and years show how difficult it is to achieve even this negative prerequisite.

It goes without saying that reunification cannot and should not be gained by force of arms. Nevertheless, both the Federal Republic and the free West can solve the German problem constructively if the Soviet Union can ultimately be convinced that self-determination in Central Europe is to its own best and enlightened interest. It would, of course, be shortsighted to assume that, from the Soviet point of view, the close ties between the Federal Republic and the West are no obstacle to reunification. On the other hand, the Federal Republic has succeeded in obtaining the consent of her Western partner countries to a policy of reunification by peaceful means. The larger the unit in which the Federal Republic is incorporated, the more easily will the West absorb the shift in the political equilibrium that will necessarily ensue from the unification of Germany. As long as the German nation is not denied the right to self-determination, and as long as the Soviet Union respects the ties between the Federal Republic and the West, the Federal Republic will always be ready, together with its allies and the Soviet Union, to search for means and ways to accommodate the legitimate interests of the Soviet Union in the matter of reunification. In terms of a global settlement, the Soviet Union would find an Atlantic Union a better forum than the Federal Republic for negotiating a *quid pro quo* for German unification. Reunification, however, seems possible only if the Soviet Union changes its attitude toward the West. Presumably this will not happen until an ideological and political evolution, inevitable in the long run, occurs in the East. And the fate of the Soviet Zone of Germany can hardly be separated from that of the other nations on this side of the Soviet western frontiers under Soviet rule. This does not imply that the solution to its problem must be identical with that to the other satellite countries. A number of solutions can conceivably be found that will make allowances for both the degree of European affinity of the East European nations and the interests of the Soviet Union. But the ideological implications of a loosening of Soviet rule over Eastern Europe pose difficult obstacles. The Western unification movement must take into account that countries such as Poland, Hungary, and Czechoslovakia are integral parts of Europe that so far have been denied the right to self-determination. Western Europe will always keep the door open for some form of association with the other East European nations, when and if they attain their freedom. This would also apply to an Atlantic Community comprising Europe and America. The Atlantic Convention in Paris affirmed its recognition of the inalienable rights of all nations to assume freely the responsibilities of self-determination and self-government, and expressed its firm belief that the problem of the captive nations of Eastern and Central Europe should be resolved in accordance with the rights and principles of both individual liberty and national self-determination. The Atlantic Community must support this position with full awareness of its political and moral importance.

EUROPE AND AMERICA—
PARTNERS IN AN ATLANTIC COMMUNITY

Many years will pass before the tasks of NATO and the OECD are fully accomplished. The faster and the more comprehensively European unification is achieved, the sooner European-American cooperation can become an institutionalized partnership. This cooperation would be greatly impeded if the negotiations between Great Britain and the EEC were to fail. A politically divided

Europe, split into numerous national states, cannot be organically integrated into an Atlantic Community unless the Community is organized along federative lines. Thus far, there is no indication of such a development. Membership in a political community presupposes fundamental agreement on common policy, a political intimacy that is possible only among more or less equal partners. Only the integration of Europe into *one* political unit will overcome the provincialism of small and medium-sized nations and prepare Europe for partnership with a first-class world power. The fact that some member countries of the OECD—e.g., Switzerland, Sweden, and Austria—cannot become members of NATO because of their neutral status, makes it likely that a future Atlantic Community will include peripheral as well as full members.[4] At the present time, no one can foresee whether other conditions will obtain, especially since the nature of neutrality is rapidly changing for a number of countries.

At any rate, achieving the goals of NATO and the OECD to the extent outlined here can eventually bring a European and American partnership to the threshold of confederation.[5] It is certainly possible that, in the end, an Atlantic Confederation may arise, particularly since the great concentration of power in the Eastern

[4] Kurt Birrenbach, "Entwurf eines Gesetzes zum Übereinkommen vom 14. Dezember 1960 über die OECD," Official Record of the House of Representatives of the German Federal Republic, June 29, 1961.

[5] Robert Strausz-Hupé, and Others, *A Forward Strategy for America* (New York: Harper & Brothers, 1961), p. 50.

bloc—once China has achieved full political and economic development—will require corresponding power in the West. Certain political developments, such as for instance the breakdown of the U.N., or other even more serious events, might conceivably accelerate Europe's political unification and the creation of confederative ties among the Atlantic nations. So long as the existing institutions of the Atlantic Community are not fully utilized and the political unification of Europe is not completed, the moment has not come to develop further concrete forms of an Atlantic Community. If we wish to consider the ways in which a partnership of Europe and North America could be organically transformed from NATO and the OECD to a more tightly integrated Atlantic Community, the experience of the European unification movement suggests the following points: Defining the future status of an Atlantic Community in terms of a federation or confederation should be avoided. To ease our task, we might seek partially to "bracket out" certain areas of the political and economic life from the sovereignty of the member states. The functional integration of individual areas of activity will facilitate the development of solidarity and render it almost inevitable that it will be continued in other fields. However, as the European experience shows, economic integration alone does not automatically bring about political integration. Thus other plans developed for the creation of a political union of European nations that preserved the sovereignty of member states—insofar as it was not yet restricted by the EEC and ECSC.[6] This is the point of the Fouchet Plan, which is likely to be approved soon by the European countries and whose principal provisions have already been made public. This proposed political union differs from confederation in the classical sense: first, in the restrictions on the sovereignty of the partner states already imposed by existing European treaties; and secondly, because the treaties contain clauses that will permit the introduction of the majority principle in certain instances. These revision clauses will become operative three years after the treaties go into force.

We conclude, then, that the experiences of the movement for European union are more applicable to the Atlantic Community problem than those of the United States or the Commonwealth. Therefore, it does not appear advisable to submit a plan for complete political integration based on a federation of the Atlantic countries—as proposed by a branch of the movement for Atlantic federation in the United States and Europe[7]—but rather to proceed along functional lines[8] and start by transferring only selected areas of political and economic life from the sovereignty of individual states to the writ of the Atlantic Community. Particular caution is called

[6] On the connection between economic and political unification, see W. Hallstein, "Wirtschaftliche Integration als Faktor politischer Einigung," in *Wirtschaft, Gesellschaft und Kultur* (Berlin, 1961); see also H. von der Groeben, "EWG und Atlantische Gemeinschaft," Speech before the Rhein-Ruhr-Club, Düsseldorf, January 22, 1962.

[7] Clarence Streit, *Union Now* and also *Freedom's Frontier* (New York: Harper & Brothers, 1940 and 1961, respectively); see also Pierre Billotte's speech before the Atlantic Convention, Paris, January, 1962.

[8] J. W. Fulbright, "For a Concert of Free Nations," *Foreign Affairs*, October, 1961.

for in one respect—the United States, not only because of its vast size and power, but also because of its far-reaching commitments in other parts of the world, can accept only limited restrictions on its sovereignty. And another factor is important: Within the movement for Western unification, European union has advanced significantly, and it now appears that West European confederate union can be forged in the foreseeable future. It would hardly be advisable to reverse such a development and to loosen West European ties in order to weave them into an Atlantic union. This reversal would be inevitable, however, if an Atlantic Community were a confederation of states rather than a federal union. It is unlikely that such a plan would be accepted by the European nations, as officials in the United States seem to realize. The recommendation made in Chicago by Mc-George Bundy on December 6, 1961, does not permit of any other interpretation. Mr. Bundy spoke of an outright partnership between the United States and a great new West European power, and there are a number of other political and military considerations that would support his plan. In the East-West conflict, the most endangered zone is Europe; given that fact, it would not seem practical to transfer the center of the Atlantic Community's political power to the periphery of that zone, i.e., to Washington, although Washington is and quite certainly will remain the military and economic power center of the Atlantic world, no matter what the developments in Western political life. Events have shown that the establishment of another center in Europe, indissolubly linked to Washington, will facilitate the solution of many political and economic problems.

As Jean Monnet put it in his speech at Dartmouth in June, 1961, the major task of the next years will be the creation of new institutions and the strengthening of existing ones (the NATO Council, the Economic and Trade Committee of the OECD, DAG, and the NATO Parliamentarians' Conference) that promise to promote political and economic cooperation between Europe and North America.[9] In order to come closer to this goal, the six European countries presently united in the EEC, together with Great Britain, might invite the United States and Canada to conclude a treaty establishing a supranational Atlantic partnership beyond NATO and OECD. Since Europe is still in the process of unification, it seems practical to wait at least until the completion of the next stage of this process as outlined in the Fouchet Plan, the establishment of institutions proposed in this plan, and the outcome of the negotiations between the EEC and Great Britain.

Under Secretary of State George Ball, in an address delivered at Bonn on April 2, 1962, said: "We have regarded a united Europe as a condition to the development of an effective Atlantic partnership. It has been necessary for Europe to move toward substantial cohesion in order to complete the foundation upon which the structure of Atlantic partnership can be erected."

Such a treaty would cover the organs of the Atlantic

[9] Cf. also Franz Joseph Strauss, "Schwelle eines neuen Zeitalters," *Rheinischer Merkur,* December 29, 1961.

Community, and the procedures through which it intends to achieve its common goals, i.e., coordination of foreign, defense, economic, agricultural, financial, trade, currency, and cultural policies. The treaty would not provide for the incorporation of the U.S. and Canada into European institutions, but rather for cooperation between them similar to that between the EEC and Great Britain in the framework of the West European Union, although the scope of that treaty is much narrower. The most important institution of the Atlantic Community—similar to that of a future European Political Union—would be an Atlantic Council of the heads of government and state in which the United States would be represented by its President and the European Political Union by its heads of government. Immediately subordinated to this Council would be an Atlantic Secretariat General consisting of the Secretary General of NATO, the Secretary General of the OECD, and a Political Secretary General for the Atlantic Council of the heads of government. This Secretariat General could be the starting point for an Atlantic executive power. Also subordinate to the Atlantic Council would be a Council of Atlantic Foreign Secretaries and a Council of Ministers of Defense, Finance, Economics, Agriculture, Trade, and Cultural Affairs.

Within such a framework, the role of NATO and the OECD would essentially depend on the progress of political integration in Europe. If Norway and Denmark should seek to become members of the EEC after Great Britain has joined and the negotiations with the EEC issue in agreement; if, after Greece, Turkey and Portugal should also join; and if all six countries, directly or indirectly, should become members of the political union (hopefully Iceland will follow the example of its Scandinavian neighbors), NATO, as a matter of course, would become an organ of the Atlantic Community, exercising the same functions as it does now. In the case of the OECD, it is unlikely that the three neutral countries—and, perhaps, Ireland and Spain—will attain the same degree of economic integration as those OECD members who are also members of NATO. The OECD would therefore be an organ of the Atlantic Community in only a limited sense, since, in addition to the two North American countries, the Community would have direct and indirect members in Europe; it seems doubtful whether the indirect members would attain a status of association as set out in Article 238 of the Rome Treaty. But at any rate, the direct members of the Atlantic Community would be so dominant that, notwithstanding this qualification, the OECD, too, could be considered an organ of the Atlantic Community. While NATO could coordinate the defense policy of the Atlantic Community, the OECD would have to coordinate its economic, finance, trade, agrarian, and currency policies. If the issues facing the Atlantic Community should exceed the limits of these two institutions, the appropriate Ministers would confer in Atlantic Councils.

If the Atlantic Community is to attain its goals, it will become necessary to introduce weighted voting in the NATO Council, in the Council of Ministers of the

OECD, and, later, in the other Councils, at least in certain selected areas. The introduction of weighted voting would constitute a breakthrough to a form of community extending beyond a purely confederative structure. (Incidentally, Article 6, Point 2, of the OECD Treaty already contains provision for a kind of majority decision. For while unanimous votes are required for any decision to be binding, and each member therefore has the right of veto, an abstention does not invalidate an otherwise unanimous decision, and it shall remain binding on those who approved it, and be put into effect at least within their national territories. Perhaps a similar provision could be included in the NATO treaty.) In any event, in the course of the development, all institutional competences would have to be regulated anew so as to avoid duplication and overlapping of authority. Parallel with these new regulations, the NATO Parliamentarians' Conference would have to be converted into a true parliament of the Atlantic Community, and not limited to strictly advisory functions.

These proposals, subject though they may be to modification, are based upon realistic considerations, no matter how wide the gap between today's fragmentary structures and the future, complete, edifice. In the course of years, the countries of the Atlantic Community are likely to accept them, although the exact form of an Atlantic federation is still obscure.

Point 12 of the Atlantic Convention of Paris proposes that the NATO governments establish a Special Governmental Commission to draw up plans within two years for the creation of a true Atlantic Community, suitably organized to meet the political, military, and economic challenges confronting the Atlantic peoples. Such a Commission would provide an organization to set in motion the development toward a true Atlantic Community.

If, in the years to come, the idea of an Atlantic Community develops in the direction outlined here, then the free West will be greatly strengthened—militarily, politically, and economically. The time may also come when we shall have to consider the possibility of common citizenship rights for all member countries of the Atlantic Community. Provision might be made for dual citizenship, whereby Atlantic citizenship would not affect national citizenship.

The Atlantic Convention recommends that all governments of the Atlantic Community that have not already done so accept the obligatory clause of the Statute of the International Court of Justice at The Hague. A true Atlantic Community is inconceivable without unanimous acceptance of this clause, which is basic to the idea of a world order under law. Accepting it would confirm the rule of law as the basis of human relationships within the framework of the Atlantic Community.

Once the Atlantic idea of today becomes the reality of tomorrow, the free West need no longer worry about the outcome of the Cold War.

Epilogue

Since the publication of the German edition of this book at the end of April, 1962, a series of welcome events both in Europe and the United States has served to speed up the developments it forecast. In Europe, negotiations between Great Britain and the Six on Britain's entry into the Common Market have reached a stage where a final agreement will be reached if good will is shown on both sides. After stormy debates over Britain's decision, the Commonwealth Conference in London tacitly accepted the inevitability of Britain's entry, though it did not formally approve the step.

Although some members of the Commonwealth voiced criticism and warnings, none of them could propose an alternative that would meet the interests of both Great Britain and the Commonwealth members concerned. The same inability to find alternatives is true of the British Labour Party, which, by imposing impossible terms at its recent annual Party Congress in Brighton, announced its opposition to Great Britain's joining the Common Market. Mr. Gaitskell's speech also offered no real alternative to Mr. Macmillan's European policy, either in regard to its economic or its political objectives. Therefore, the Prime Minister can feel that his policy toward Europe has been justified. The clarity and vigor with which the British Government defended its European policy at the Marlborough House Conference should leave no doubt about Britain's determination, at least while under a Conservative government, to consider itself a member of the European Community. Indeed, the debates with the Commonwealth clearly showed that the principal motive underlying Britain's decision to join the Common Market is political; hence it is certain that Britain will want to join a European political union after entry into the Common Market. In view of this determination, a breakdown of the negotiations between Great Britain and the Common Market would have extremely serious consequences.

At the same time, President de Gaulle's visit to West Germany showed the world that Franco-German reconciliation is now a reality. This development is as significant as the historic change in Britain's policy toward Europe. Close ties between France and Germany are the cornerstone for the unity of Continental Europe. These ties, however, should not be considered the alternative to a larger European unity. Once Great Britain has joined the Common Market, all the obstacles that have blocked a European political union will disappear.

During the first phase of European political development, the French conception of a union of European nations will be the most practical. This conception is outlined in the second draft version of the Fouchet Plan, as amended according to suggestions by other member states. But if that union is to be realized, a common, even if embryonic, organ modeled on the European Commission of the Common Market should be part of a framework of a political union. For, as Jean Monnet has stated, continuous dialogues between an independent European political entity and the national governments will be the real federating force in Europe.

The European part of a future Atlantic Community has been greatly strengthened in recent months, but two events in the United States have also helped to prepare for it. The first was President Kennedy's speech on July 4, 1962, in Philadelphia, in which he proclaimed the doctrine of interdependence and offered to form an Atlantic partnership with the united Europe of tomorrow. Let us hope that the peoples on each side of the Atlantic will always keep in mind the significance of this "grand design" and of the responsibilities it imposes.

The other important American event was the passage of the Trade Expansion Act. That the opposition to this law was insignificant suggests that political developments have begun to reflect the necessities of modern economic life and adjust to the revolutionary changes of the postwar period.

Certainly some time will elapse before negotiations for a trade partnership between the United States and a Common Market including Great Britain can start. The difficulties that the negotiators will face will be apparent to anyone familiar with the issues, but if the negotiations come to a happy conclusion, the free West will experience a new birth of strength and confidence.

October, 1962

APPENDIX A

Declaration of Paris

We, the citizen delegates to the Atlantic Convention of NATO nations, meeting in Paris, January 8–20, 1962, are convinced that our survival as free men, and the possibility of progress for all men, demand the creation of a true Atlantic Community within the next decade, and therefore submit this declaration of our convictions:

Preamble

The Atlantic peoples are heir to a magnificent civilization whose origins include the early achievements of the Near East, the classical beauty of Greece, the juridical sagacity of Rome, the spiritual power of our religious traditions, and the humanism of the Renaissance. Its latest flowering, the discoveries of modern science, allow an extraordinary mastery of the forces of nature.

While our history has too many pages of tragedy and error, it has also evolved principles transcending the vicissitudes of history, such as the supremacy of law, respect for individual rights, social justice, and the duty of generosity.

Thanks to that civilization and to the common characteristics with which it stamps the development of the peoples participating in it, the nations of the West do in fact constitute a powerful cultural and moral community.

But the time has now come when the Atlantic countries

must close their ranks if they wish to guarantee their security against the Communist menace and ensure that their unlimited potentialities shall develop to the advantage of all men of good will.

A true Atlantic Community must extend to the political, military, economic, moral, and cultural fields. The evolution we contemplate will contribute to the diversity of achievements and aspirations which constitute the cultural splendor and intellectual wealth of our peoples.

The Atlantic Convention, keeping this ideal constantly in view, recommends the following measures which, in its opinion, would foster the necessary cohesion of the West, would bring the final objective closer, and should be adopted forthwith by the governments concerned.

Summary of Recommendations

1. To define the principles on which our common civilization is based and to consult about ways of ensuring respect for these principles.

2. To create, as an indispensable feature of a true Atlantic Community, a permanent High Council at the highest political level, to concert and plan, and in agreed cases to decide policy on matters of concern to the Community as a whole. Pending the establishment of the Council, the Convention recommends that the North Atlantic Council be strengthened through the delegation of additional responsibilities.

3. To develop the NATO Parliamentarians' Conference into a consultative Assembly which would review the work of all Atlantic institutions and make recommendations to them.

4. To establish an Atlantic High Court of Justice, to de-

cide specified legal controversies which may arise under the Treaties.

5. To harmonize political, military, and economic policy on matters affecting the Community as a whole.

6. That the North Atlantic Council treat the development of an agreed NATO policy with respect to nuclear weapons as a matter of urgency.

7. That it welcomes the development, progress and prospective expansion of the European economic institutions, and the spirit of President Kennedy's statement that a trade partnership be formed between the United States and the European Economic Community, the basis of an Atlantic Economic Community, open to other nations of the free world.

8. That the Atlantic nations, acknowledging the right of every people to freedom, independence, and pursuit of happiness, cooperate on a larger scale with the developing nations in their economic programs, through direct and multi-lateral action; through the acceleration of investments; and especially through measures which would increase both the volume and value of their exports, including special tariff concessions for their exports.

9. That the Atlantic Community take steps to help improve all their economies, so that the proportionate economic and social potential of all will be less unequal.

10. That the Atlantic nations, noting the destruction of the national independence and the human rights of many peoples in Eastern Central Europe, reaffirms its belief that the problem of these captive nations should be resolved in accordance with the principles of both individual liberty and national self-determination.

11. To create an Atlantic Council for youth, education,

and culture in order to draw up Atlantic plans for exchanges of young people, students, and teachers, and for the purposes of scientific and cultural collaboration.

12. That the NATO Governments promptly establish a Special Governmental Commission to draw up plans within two years for the creation of a true Atlantic Community, suitably organized to meet the political, military, and economic challenges of this era.

RESOLUTIONS

We, the delegates to the Atlantic Convention of NATO Nations, in meeting assembled, taking note of the recommendations of the NATO Parliamentarians' Conference of November 17, 1961, that an organized Atlantic Community be created, have adopted the following documents:

Part I—Political and Economic Questions
A. Special Governmental Commission to Propose Organizational Changes

Call upon the Governments of the NATO countries to draw up plans within two years for the creation of an Atlantic Community suitably organized to meet the political, military, and economic challenges of this era. To this end they should, within the earliest practicable period, appoint members to a Special Governmental Commission on Atlantic unity. The Commission should study the organization of the Atlantic Community, particularly in the light of the recommendations of this Convention, and it should be instructed to propose such reforms and simplifications of existing institutions and such new institutions as may be required.

Appendix A

B. Institutions

1. Recommend, as an indispensable feature of a true Atlantic Community, the creation at the highest political level, of a Permanent High Council, whose competence would extend to political, economic, military, and cultural matters. Such a Council, assisted by a Secretariat, would not only prepare and concert policies on current questions and, in defined cases, decide them by a weighted, qualified majority vote, but would also undertake long-term planning and propose initiatives on matters of concern to the Community. All members of the Community would be represented on the Council.

Whether this High Council be a new institution or a development of the North Atlantic Council should be a matter of recommendation by the Special Governmental Commission. In any event, however, pending the establishment of the Atlantic Community, the members of the Convention urgently request their governments to reinforce and develop the North Atlantic Treaty Organization as a political center. To this end, the Convention recommends that the North Atlantic Council be strengthened through the delegation of additional jurisdiction. Where authority for decision is delegated to the North Atlantic Council by governments, it should employ a weighted majority vote.

2. Propose that the NATO Parliamentarians' Conference be developed into a consultative Atlantic Assembly, to meet at stated intervals, or upon the call of its President or otherwise, to receive reports regularly transmitted to it by the Secretaries General of other Atlantic bodies; to raise questions for and to consider, debate, and review the work of all Atlantic institutions, and make recommendations to other Atlantic bodies and governments on questions of concern

to the Atlantic Community. A permanent secretariat and an annual budget should be provided for the Atlantic Assembly to insure continuity. In certain defined cases, recommendations should be by weighted majority vote. Members of the Atlantic Assembly would be selected by member governments in accordance with their constitutional procedures. They need not necessarily be Parliamentarians. The members thus chosen would have the power to elect a limited number of additional members of equal status.

3. Recommend the creation of a High Court of Justice, reserved to the Atlantic Community, in order to settle legal differences between members and between members and the organizations arising from the interpretation and application of treaties.

C. Policies

The institutions of the Atlantic Community should harmonize those policies of its members affecting the interests of the Community as a whole, and contribute to the development of Community methods in planning, considering, and executing such policies.

1. A primary objective is the continuing expression through national and international action of an overriding community of national interests in political and military policy. Closer and more effective action in this field should not await the growth of Community institutions (see Paragraph 2, above); the development of an agreed NATO policy with respect to nuclear weapons should, among other immediate problems, be treated as a matter of urgency by the North Atlantic Council.

2. A second cardinal policy objective is to realize the opportunities for economic progress available through the

creation and development of the Atlantic Community. The expanding European Economic Community is an economic advantage not only for its members, but for North America and the free world as well. The Convention welcomes the spirit of President Kennedy's recent statement that a trade partnership be formed between the United States and the European Economic Community. We hope that the negotiations envisaged by President Kennedy succeed in establishing a relationship which would constitute the nucleus of an Atlantic Economic Community, within the framework of Community institutions, and open to all other qualified countries. Such a development would be of advantage to all countries, and particularly to those which participate directly in it. Among the fruits of this expanding Community would be its stimulus to competition, investment, and more rapid growth in the mass markets appropriate to the modern technological age, with progressive reductions in tariffs and other barriers to trade.

3. Another important goal of the Atlantic nations is to cooperate with those developing nations which wish to do so in their efforts to overcome the burden of poverty, which may well be that of a falling per capita income in some countries. The Convention recommends that the Atlantic Community increase its already considerable participation in development programs of this kind, through direct financial and technical measures; through increased shares in United Nations programs, OECD programs, and other multilateral efforts; and above all through policies which favor commerce with and investment in the development countries, such as the abolition of tariffs on tropical and primary products, and the reduction and, under agreed circumstances, even the eventual abolition of tariffs on their other

products. The Convention also recommends the development of equitable and agreed programs for the acceleration of investments, and for the protection of investors against political risks.

4. An important goal of the Atlantic Community's economic policies should be to help raise the standard of living and the level of economic activity of the different segments of the Atlantic Community, so that the proportional economic and social potential of all the members will be relatively less unequal.

5. In view of the hundreds of millions of hungry people alive today, and the prospect that, if the present trends continue, there will be three thousand million more people added to the population in the next generation, the Convention recommends that the Atlantic Community should address itself forthwith to the population problem.

6. Since Soviet expansion has destroyed the effective national independence of many peoples in Eastern and Central Europe, denying to their individual members the free exercise of their religious rights and democratic liberties— with all the attendant injurious effects upon the general climate of European security and progress, the Convention affirms its recognition of the inalienable rights of all nations to assume freely the responsibilities of self-determination and self-government, and expresses its firm belief that the problem of the captive nations of Eastern and Central Europe should be resolved in accordance with the rights and principles of both individual liberty and national self-determination.

7. As most governments of the Atlantic Community countries have accepted the obligatory clause of the Statute of the International Court of Justice at The Hague, the

Convention recommends that all members of the Atlantic Community accept this obligatory clause.

Part II—Moral and Cultural Questions
A. The Atlantic Convention of NATO nations

Declares that the basic moral and spiritual principles upon which the lives and acts of the nations forming the Atlantic Community are based are as follows:

1. The purpose of political and economic institutions is the protection and promotion of the rights, liberties, and duties which enable every human being to fulfill his or her spiritual vocation;

2. Liberty is inseparable from responsibility, which implies recognition of a moral law to which men, as individuals and in groups, are subject;

3. Liberty is inseparable from the duties of men toward one another, which implies the obligation to ensure that all men gradually attain physical and moral well-being;

4. Liberty is inseparable from tolerance, which recognizes the right to free discussion of all opinions which are not in violation of the very principles of civilization;

5. There can be no freedom without variety, the natural result of the different origins and varying achievements of different peoples in all fields. But this variety should not entail disunity. On the contrary, retaining the common factors, it should become the permanent force impelling the peoples of our Western civilization to unite;

6. Freedom is inseparable from the spirit of objective truth, which must restore to words the exact meaning they have in the Free World.

And therefore *invites* member countries:

1. To defend and promote the values and principles of civilization by means of education, publications, lectures, radio, the cinema, and television;

2. To uphold in their conduct with all nations the ethics and values of Western civilization and by their example to impress on others that discord and disunity result when they are not observed;

3. To defend these values and principles against intellectual and moral subversion within the Community;

4. To try to establish an atmosphere of mutual understanding between the members of the Atlantic Community, appreciating to the full the riches of their diversity;

5. To demonstrate to all peoples that respect for these values and principles can alone make a technological civilization an instrument for improving the physical and moral well-being of mankind;

Reconstruction of the Acropolis: To decide that the Acropolis shall become the symbol of our culture and the shrine of our Alliance and to call upon governments to consider how this resolution might be given concrete form.

B. The Atlantic Convention of NATO nations

Considering that a major obstacle to the formation of real European and Atlantic Communities is the difference in language and therefore in mentalities and ways of thinking;

Considering that this language barrier is particularly prejudicial to the scientific cooperation upon which the Western potential depends:

Invites the Governments of NATO nations, and such other countries as may be inspired by the same ideal, to convene an Atlantic Council consisting of Ministers of

Education, Ministers for Scientific Affairs, cultural and educational authorities, and representatives of universities and scientific research organizations, with a view to:

1. Determining the comprehensive aims of an education likely to promote the ideals and purposes of the Atlantic Community, studying ways and means of implementing the principles laid down, and periodically reviewing the results achieved.

2. Organizing: a bold Atlantic Plan for Youth and Education with the aim of furthering the study of languages and the widest possible exchange of students, teachers and youth leaders, and of workers in industry and agriculture, a program of scientific cooperation among the scientists and the scientific institutions of the countries of the Community, both of the above being financed by all participating nations.

Within the framework of the above recommendations, the Convention *draws the attention of governments* to the following points:

a. Alongside the study and use of foreign languages, it is essential that mutual understanding be developed between men with different ways of thinking from all parts of the free world, including those of the emergent nations. This program should in the first place benefit university students, as many as possible of whom should be enabled to spend at least one year of their course in a university or other advanced training establishment where teaching is in a language other than their own.

However, in the case of the most promising citizens of the emergent nations this program should have a special priority, since their intellectual hunger must be satisfied at all costs.

Steps will have to be taken to ensure that such periods spent at foreign universities or other establishments do not prejudice the career of the student concerned but rather confer advantages upon him in the form of either a degree valid in his own country or a new type of degree specially created for the purpose of enabling him, for instance, to exercise his profession either in his own country or in that where he has completed one or more years of study, always providing that his knowledge of the two languages is sufficient.

b. It is to be hoped that, in the future, those who have pursued such a course of training, which would subsequently be supplemented by exchanges of civil servants between Atlantic nations, will be given priority in selection for posts as officials required to take part in international negotiations.

c. It should be made possible for teachers, and particularly university teachers, research workers and curators of museums and art galleries, either to be seconded periodically to equivalent foreign organizations, or to establish close contacts with them. Although it may not be immediately possible for all Atlantic Community countries, the introduction of the system of the "sabbatical year" for professors and research workers would be generally desirable.

d. In the field of scientific documentation and cooperation, it would be necessary to supplement existing organs by setting up a Scientific Documentation Center responsible, among other things, for the translation and distribution of the principal articles, reports, and other publications appearing throughout the world, and which have not yet been distributed by other agencies. The Committee considers this a most urgent matter.

e. The "pairing-off" of universities and other advanced educational establishments of different languages within the Community should be encouraged and intensified.

f. The establishment and exchange of comparable statistics on education and research in the Atlantic Community countries should be assured.

C. Recommends that these proposals be studied further by the Atlantic Institute to assist in the accomplishment of these tasks in cooperation with existing agencies, such as the Council for Cultural Cooperation of the Council of Europe to avoid duplication of effort.

GENERAL RESOLUTION

The Atlantic Convention of NATO Nations requests its President to forward the foregoing Declaration and Resolutions to the NATO Council and to the NATO Parliamentarians' Conference at the earliest possible date, and that the delegates to this Convention report the same to their respective Governments or Legislative authorities at their earliest convenience.

APPENDIX B

Second Declaration of Atlantic Unity
(Adopted by the Sponsors, April, 1962)

We, the undersigned citizens of Belgium, Canada, Denmark, France, Germany, Greece, Iceland, Italy, Luxembourg, the Netherlands, Norway, Turkey, the United Kingdom, and the United States address this APPEAL FOR ATLANTIC UNITY *to our fellow citizens and to our governments.*

We believe:

That sovereignty of the individual and freedom under law are mankind's most precious political heritage.

That the bastion of human freedom is the Atlantic Community.

That this bastion remains in grave peril.

That only by our unity can we preserve the liberties we enjoy and only by our example will they appeal to all mankind.

International Communism believes in unity through force; its aim is a monolithic tyranny; it is determined to destroy us. Its threat to freedom is not only military but also political, ideological and economic. It is not confined to Europe or the Atlantic but is world wide. We must be united in our relevant policies on all fronts and in all areas.

We, therefore, mutually pledge our support to each

other as faithful friends who share a common cultural and spiritual heritage and the institutions and processes of democracy. We dedicate our efforts to develop our alliance into a true Atlantic Community to insure that these concepts shall not perish from the earth.

We call on our governments to undertake without delay these measures to establish a true Atlantic Community, the first five of which were unanimously recommended by the Atlantic Convention of NATO Nations at Paris in January, 1962; to:

1. Establish a governmental commission on Atlantic Unity to draw up a Charter for an Atlantic Community suitably organized to meet the challenges of this era.

2. Create a permanent High Council which should act in defined cases by a weighted majority vote on matters of common concern.

3. Develop the NATO Parliamentarians' Conference into a consultative Atlantic Assembly which would review the work of all Atlantic institutions and make recommendations to them.

4. Form a trade partnership between the European Economic Community and North America as a basis for an Atlantic Economic Community, but open to all other qualified nations of the free world.

5. Establish an Atlantic High Court of Justice to decide specific legal controversies which might arise under Community treaties.

6. Promote measures to ensure more effective defense including further development of a unified Atlantic command; a common strategy both inside and outside the Atlantic area; greater standardization and a

more rational production of arms and equipment; and defense contributions fairly shared among our respective countries.

7. Support and expand the Atlantic Institute as an intellectual and spiritual center for the Atlantic Community.

Only by a united and integrated effort can we provide economic aid to, and markets for, developing countries on the scale required.

Inspired by the contributions made in the past by our separate nations, we can follow a glorious destiny by joining our present strength.